The Fortune Telling Handbook

THE
FORTUNE
TELLING
HANDBOOK

Viv Foster

Grange
BOOKS

AN OCEANA BOOK

Published by Grange Books
an imprint of Grange Books Plc
The Grange
Kingsnorth Industrial Estate
Hoo, nr. Rochester
Kent ME3 9ND
www.grangebooks.co.uk

ISBN 1-84013-905-6

This book was produced by
Quantum Books
6 Blundell Street
London N7 9BH

QUMFTH2

Manufactured in Singapore by
Universal Graphics Pte Ltd
Printed in China by
CT Printing Ltd

Contents

Introduction   6

History of Astrology   13

Western Astrology   21

Chinese Astrology   35

Signs of the Zodiac   49

Tarot   139

Necromancy   157

Palmistry   161

Numerology   171

Crystallomancy   179

Cartomancy   183

Dreams   193

I Ching   199

Other Methods of
    Fortune Telling   207

Superstitions   217

Glossary   220

Index   222

Introduction

Astrology's roots are inextricably linked to the development of mythologies in early cultures all over the world.

In the British Isles, Stonehenge, which dates back in part to 3000 B.C. is thought to have been used to predict the eclipses of the sun and moon – events that still have great astrological significance today. Other ancient monuments for forecasting are found scattered throughout the world, notably in China, India, Japan and the United States.

The modern, 12-sign zodiac emerged in Babylonia around the fifth century B.C. This system divided the heavens into twelve 300 sections consisting of one sign each. In the fourth century B.C., Greece became a major centre of astrology and as Alexander the Great conquered much of Asia Minor, Egypt, Babylonia, Iran and

Astrology has always been a powerful symbolic language. This beautiful painting is from Turkey, dating back to the sixteenth century. It depicts the strong association between the watery crab and the moon.

Nostradamus, the legendary French prophet, claimed to be able to see into the future and cloaked his predictions in intriguing and ambiguous verse. The exact meaning of much of his writing is still hotly debated today.

India, Greek ideas spread in these areas. Eventually, Egypt became a centre of astrology and the ideas that developed there formed the origins of modern Western astrology. India and China have separate traditions of astrology that evolved independently.

However, most early astrology, wherever it was practiced, focused mainly on the affairs of royalty and the state; it was only much later that astrologers began to apply their readings to the lives of ordinary people.

In Western civilization, astrology had been accepted by the Church and the leading philosophers of the time up until the seventeenth century. However, its popularity and credibility started to decline as scientific thought became more established and various religious movements began to denounce alternative beliefs. As knowledge of the solar system increased, so doubt was cast on the belief that human life could be influenced by the planets.

ASTROLOGY TODAY

Although astrology continues to be attacked and discredited in the West, the twentieth century witnessed something of a resurgence, perhaps as people decided that neither science nor religion has all the answers to life's deepest questions.

In the East, astrology has had a profound effect on all aspects of society from the earliest times, and this trend continues unabated. The Eastern mind has always been more open to astrology, and despite the rise of modern science and technology, mystical ways of interpreting the world are regarded as equally important.

On a universal level, astrology's deep roots in the psyche of humanity show no signs of disappearing. On the contrary, media coverage seems to grow each year, particularly with the turn of the millennium.

An eighteenth century Tibetan manuscript showing the 12 animals of the Chinese zodiac.

7

There is a fascination with the future which draws most people – young and old, male and female, of every colour and belief – into spending some time and money on trying to discover what is going to happen to them, or what decisions they should make. (In Christian countries this is despite clear warnings against fortune telling in the Bible, which says, for example, 'Do not practise divination or sorcery', *Leviticus* 19: 6).

You are one of those people, or else you would not be reading this book. You probably do not know a great deal about the different methods of fortune telling (or divination). You could consult a professional who might give you a tarot reading, scrutinize your palm, cast your birth chart or look into a crystal ball for symbols of your future. Or, instead, you might be able to predict the future for yourself, and this book will teach you something about the current methods of fortune telling. It sets out a range of possibilities. In some cases it will give you enough information for you to try the system for yourself, at home. In other cases, where the method is very complicated or requires expensive equipment or a particular talent, it will help you to understand what is involved in the method.

Fortune telling has an extremely long history – longer than any written records show. Hundreds of methods have been used and discarded over the centuries. For example, it is rare these days for anybody to kill an animal in order to read fortunes from its still-warm entrails. Such methods are ignored here. This book will concentrate on the 11 major and a few minor methods still widely used in the West today.

DINNER PARTY FORTUNE TELLING

Some minor methods are easily overlooked, or else are not thought of as 'proper' fortune telling. For example, there are fortune cookies, common in American Chinese restaurants but rare in British Chinese restaurants. These are small pastry cases, folded over and cooked hard, each containing a strip of paper bearing a one-line homily or piece of advice, rather than an actual predictive fortune. Examples of such fortune cookie slips are 'Be on the alert for new opportunities' and 'Proceed with caution'. Obviously, nobody is meant to take the advice in fortune cookies very seriously.

A fortune-telling system need not be difficult or complex or take much time. It takes only a second to pull a fortune out of a fortune cookie. It takes only slightly longer to carry out some of the methods involving candles. The simplest is really just an omen. At a dinner party or similar gatherings where several people are sitting around a table, light a new candle and place it in the centre.

Note which side the molten wax first begins to run down, because it signifies bad luck for the person sitting at that side of the table. Slightly more formal, and requiring some preparation, are two other candle methods, lithomancy and lychnomancy. (The word-ending 'mancy' means 'fortune telling by means of',) 'Litho-' comes from 'lithos', the ancient Greek word for a stone, while 'lycho-'comes from 'lynchnos', the Greek for a lamp.

LYCHNOMANCY

Set up three ordinary wax candles in a triangle, preferably in three identical candlesticks or holders. This should be done in a room with its doors and windows closed and no draughts to affect the burning of flames. Then turn off all other lights in the room (you will need a small torch or perhaps another candle, already lit, to see your way) and light the three candles with the same match. Clues to the future can be read in the behaviour of the candle flames.

- If one candle seems to burn more brightly than the other two it means success and good fortune for you.

- If the end of any of the three wicks displays a brightly shining point it is a lucky omen.

- If a flame moves from side to side it indicates that you will soon travel.

- If there are sparks rising from a candle you will need to be cautious.

- If the flame of one of the candles seems to twist and spiral it means that your enemies are plotting against you.

- If a flame rises and falls it suggests there is approaching danger.

- If one of the candles is extinguished suddenly and without good reason it is a prediction of great disaster.

LITHOMANCY

Scatter a few precious or semi-precious stones on a flat surface – they must be in a variety of colours. Light a candle and set it up in the middle of them. Turn off all other lights to aid your concentration and close your eyes. When you open them, note the colour of the first stone which catches your eye by reflecting the candle light towards you.

A blue stone means good luck; a colourless one, happiness and success; green means a wish granted; red means romance; claret means a marriage; turquoise indicates an opportunity; yellow means unfaithfulness; grey is for sadness; violet for grief; purple for a quarrel and black for bad luck.

RUNES

About 1,800 years ago the runic alphabet came into being among the Norse peoples of northern Europe. It was said to be a gift from Odin, chief of the Norse gods.

One of its uses was as a predictive device, carefully controlled by rune masters. The last rune masters lived in Iceland in the seventeenth century, and it was only about ten years ago that runes were re-introduced for divination.

Although slight variations exist, the sets of runes on sale today are fairly traditional. Sets consist of 25 rune stones (occasionally only 22). Each, except for a blank, is marked with a symbol of the runic alphabet, made up of straight lines because it was easier to carve straight lines into stone rather than curves.

RUNE POSITIONS

For reading purposes, the rune stones should be placed face down and shuffled, then 13 chosen and arranged in a clock face, proceeding anticlockwise from 9 o'clock, with the 13 in the centre. These positions are concerned with:

1 personality
2 material wealth
3 family
4 home
5 self-expression
6 health and the environment
7 love and marriage
8 inheritance
9 education
10 job, status
11 pleasures, friendship
12 psychic feelings
13 the questioner

Note that runes are upright if their tops are closest to the centre.

RUNE MEANINGS

R means that the rune is reversed or inverted

Feoh property, wealth, fulfilment, growth.
R loss.
Ur strength masculinity, skill.
R weakness, missed chances.
Thorn protection of all kinds.
R wrong decision, jealousy.
Os authority, father figures.
R problems with superiors.
Rad movement, change.
R problems with travel or changes.
Ken warmth, love, status.
R lack of warmth or direction.
Gyfu gift, opportunity.
R loss, swindle, illness.

Wyn joy, happiness, luck.
R over-emotion, depression.
Hagal sudden change, good or bad
R delay, disaster.
Nyd self-preservation, needs.
R tension, stress
Is obstacles, stagnation.
R fear, coldness, no hope
Ger end of a cycle, renewal
R the same
Eoh flexibility, cunning.
R indecision, withdrawal
Peorth occult knowledge, hope.
R disappointment, fear.
Eohls artistry, culture, pleasure.
R a lack of these.
Sygel life force, healing, fame.
R the same, over-used.

Tir energy, heroism, romance.
R weakness, love spurned.
Beorc fertility, beginnings.
R barrenness, delay, illness.
Eow travel, animals, ideas.
R problems with these.
Man authority, consult professionals.
R trouble with these.
Lagu intuition, change, fertility
R paranoia, blood.
Ing fertility, fruition, solution.
R restriction, illness.
Daeg face values, clarity, success.
R the same.
Ethel legacy, gift, help, problems with property.
The blank rune fate, hidden things; its meaning is partly determined by adjacent runes.

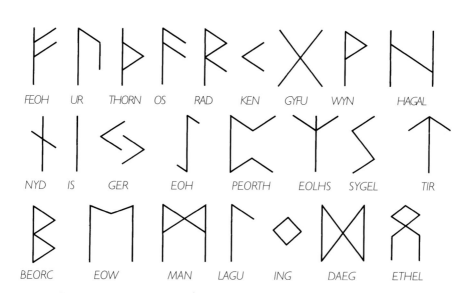

FEOH UR THORN OS RAD KEN GYFU WYN HAGAL

NYD IS GER EOH PEORTH EOLHS SYGEL TIR

BEORC EOW MAN LAGU ING DAEG ETHEL

11

Jupiter

BABILONIA SEV BABILON

History
of Astrology

Astrology began over 5,000 and possibly as much as 7,000 years ago, the first exact science to be studied by mankind. It was probably born in Ur of the Chaldees, a city of Sumer, a part of Mesopotamia north of the Persian Gulf, and it was confined to divining the omens for king and nation only. North of Sumer was Babylonia and it was in those two countries that the foundations were laid from which the modern systems have descended.

History of Astrology

The fixed constellations seemed unchanging, but in the clear atmosphere of Mesopotamia, where observation was assisted by wide expanses of flat landscape, the movement of those heavenly bodies which seemed to traverse regular paths was noticed, the planets we call Mercury, Venus, Mars, Jupiter and Saturn were known to the Sumerians and the Babylonians.

The belt of the zodiac in which the paths of the planets mainly lay (though they occasionally wandered outside it, when they were thought to be resting in their 'houses') may have been known for millennia, though most modern scholarship ascribes its recognition to Greek science of the sixth and fifth centuries B.C. The Sumerians identified Venus with Innin or Inanna, the Lady of Heaven, and the Babylonians regarded her as Ishtar, goddess of war and carnage in her appearance as the Morning Star, but of love, procreation, fertility, gentleness and luxury when she shone as the Evening Star. She was the daughter of Sin, the Moon god, and sister of Utu or Shamash, deity of the Sun. Nergal, god of war and destruction, and ruler of the underworld, was appropriately the red planet, Mars; Mercury was Babylonian Nabu; Jupiter was Marduk and Saturn Ninib.

ABOVE *A Babylonian boundary stone, c.1120 B.C., recording a gift of land, bears the symbols of gods invoked to protect the deed.*

LEFT *This cylinder seal of the Scribe Adda, c. 2400–2200 B.C. shows, among other deities, the Sun-God, Shamash (on the right).*

Reports of earthly phenomena apparently resulting from the movements of heaven's gods, though most of them were on the level of meteorological forecasts, were recorded in writings known as the Enunia Anu Enlil tablets, dating from the beginning of the fourth millennium B.C. Records of predictions followed, first of events such as wars and floods, later birth horoscopes of individual kings, some of which still exist on cuneiform tablets.

Eastwards, Mesopotamian astrology penetrated to India around the sixth century B.C. and to China and Indo-China soon after (though there

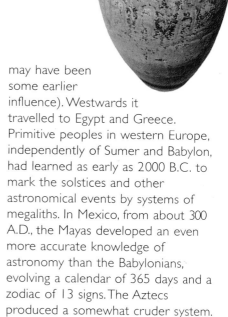

RIGHT *A Chinese zodiacal vase of the fifth to sixth centuries A.D. decorated with the images of 12 animals representing the months of the year.*

may have been some earlier influence). Westwards it travelled to Egypt and Greece. Primitive peoples in western Europe, independently of Sumer and Babylon, had learned as early as 2000 B.C. to mark the solstices and other astronomical events by systems of megaliths. In Mexico, from about 300 A.D., the Mayas developed an even more accurate knowledge of astronomy than the Babylonians, evolving a calendar of 365 days and a zodiac of 13 signs. The Aztecs produced a somewhat cruder system.

LEFT *A Mayan manuscript from Mexico. In the clear atmosphere of their location, the Mayas developed a sophisticated astronomical system.*

THE IMPORTANT EARLY TEXTS

The Greeks identified the planets with deities very similar in character to those of the Babylonians. Ishtar, the Morning and Evening Star, became Aphrodite, in Roman culture Venus. Nabu turned into Greek Hermes, Roman Mercury, messenger of the gods. Through the conquests of Alexander the Great (356–323 B.C.), Greek ideas spread throughout the ancient world, but the Greeks themselves were exposed to foreign influence. In 280 B.C. Bedosus, a Chaldean priest, brought astrology to Greece.

Egypt, however, had developed her own astronomy long before. From possibly 2000 B.C. she had developed a calendar which the Greeks later made their own. The Persians introduced astrology to Egypt in the sixth century B.C., with the result that the Egyptians evolved a form of astral religion which eventually influenced both Greece and Rome. Thirty-six stars named decans were selected, rising at ten-day intervals, each governed by a spirit. The ten-day periods evolved into ten-degree subdivisions of the twelve 30° zodiacal signs. In about 150 B.C. a treatise by a fictitious priest, Petosiris, and king, Nechepso, ascribed each day of the week to a planet. Even more important was the collection of texts made between 50 B.C. and 150 A.D., attributed to Hermes, the Greek Mercury and Egyptian Thoth. That ordinary though well-to-do men were concerned with astrology is shown by the fact that horoscopes were sometimes inscribed on tombs.

LEFT *A seventeenth-century Chinese painting of a group studying the yin-yang symbol.*

BELOW *The interior of an Egyptian coffin, second century A.D., showing the goddess Nut and the signs of the zodiac.*

ABOVE *Ptolemy (Claudius Ptolemaeus), established the theory accepted until the fifteenth century that the earth was the centre of the universe.*

LEFT *A scribe presenting a copy of the Tetrabiblas, by Ptolemy, to King Henry VI.*

The Chinese were probably the first people to develop astronomy apart from astrology, which they used to forecast events. They divided the sky into five 'palaces', a central region around the pole and four equatorial divisions corresponding to the four seasons. 12 signs – Tiger, Hare, Dragon, Serpent, Horse, Sheep, Monkey, Hen, Dog, Pig, Rat and Ox – alternatively possessing the quality of positive *Yang* (masculinity, light and motion) and negative *Yin* (femininity, darkness and repose), were based on divisions of the equator (not of the sky, as with the zodiac).

The complicated and apparently scientific system that was to be the ancestor of European astrology was meanwhile being developed by the Greeks from their own genius combined with Babylonian and Egyptian elements. Philosophy, medicine and religion all supported it. The Stoic doctrine of universal 'sympathy' between the microcosm (man) and the macrocosm (the universe), expressed in the dictum used later when Stoicism no longer existed, 'as above, so below' – and astrology seemed made for each other. Mithraism, so great a rival of Christianity that a toss of the historical coin might have made it, rather than Christianity, the religion of Europe, initiated its worshippers, who in their rites wore masks representing the animals of the zodiac, into successive mysteries representing the soul's journey through the seven planetary realms. Gnosticism in its many forms and some of the mystery religions were based on very similar concepts. Melothesis, the 'science' that teaches that the stars and zodiac dominate parts of the body, became part of standard medical practice.

In Rome the official augurs opposed astrology when it arrived there during the second century BC, but the populace welcomed 'Chaldeans' who told their fortunes by the stars. The Roman emperors disliked astrology, regarding it as a possible weapon to be used by would-be usurpers of their thrones. It found a supporter in the person of the Neoplatonist philosopher Plotinus, who settled in Rome in 241 A.D.

RIGHT *The birth of Jesus announced to the shepherds by a host of angels and the Star of Bethlehem. Astrology is of course immediately relevant to the Christian dilemma concerning predestination and free will.*

In spite of a number of references in the Old Testament to astrology, Judaism had little time for it even though it recorded the fact that 'the stars in their courses fought against' Sisera. According to Christianity, Judaism's largest and most successful heresy, the coming of Christ, broke the control of the planets over human fate. One Christian view was that the star of Bethlehem changed the old order; another that it was the constellation of Cassiopeia, which produced an unusually bright star every 300 years and was known to the ancients as 'The Woman with Child'. Furthermore, Cassiopeia was the presiding constellation of Syria/Palestine, and it was natural for the Magi, who were astrologers, not kings, to follow the sign that proclaimed to them that a woman of Palestine had brought forth a royal son.

Early Christianity was sometimes tolerant of, sometimes hostile to, astrology. *The Clementine Recognitions* (second century) stated that God created the celestial bodies to be an indication of things past, present and future and that Abraham had recognized the creator from the stars. Hostile Christian writers, including Augustine, attacked astrology with a double-edged sword of an argument – it was either erroneous or, if right, owed its accuracy to the devil.

The Jewish *Sepher Yetsirah* (Book of Creation, written *c.* 500 A.D.), one of the classics of the Jewish mystical system known as the *Kabbalah*, and the *Zohar* (Book of Splendor) both affected European thought and both revealed faith in celestial influence.

Astrology all but disappeared in Europe during the Dark Ages but was kept alive by the Mohammedans. In the eighth century the Caliph Al Mansur founded a school of astrology in Baghdad with the practical aims of catching thieves, recovering lost possessions and determining the best time to start enterprises. When learning revived in the eleventh and twelfth centuries Christendom accepted Arabian astrological treatises because of their Aristotelian flavour. Aquinas (*c.* 1126–1274) gave the definitive Christian compromise with astrology and made it acceptable. Since the stars influence human appetites, which few men can resist, their forecasts are mostly correct; but those morally strong enough to resist can

negate their predictions.

Astrology/astronomy (for the two did not really part company until the seventeenth century), reached its zenith during the Renaissance, when the New Learning (of which much was old rediscovered) permeated to the masses. Famous scholars wrote astrological treatises, of whom the most eminent was the Swiss Paracelsus (1492–1541) who believed that man's inner nature corresponded to the universe. He could, however, resist the influence of stars and planets.

Some popes (for example Julius II, Leo X and Paul III) and potentates favoured astrologers. Catherine de Medici patronized the famous Nostradamus (1503-1566), and Elizabeth I of England Dr John Dee (1527-1608).

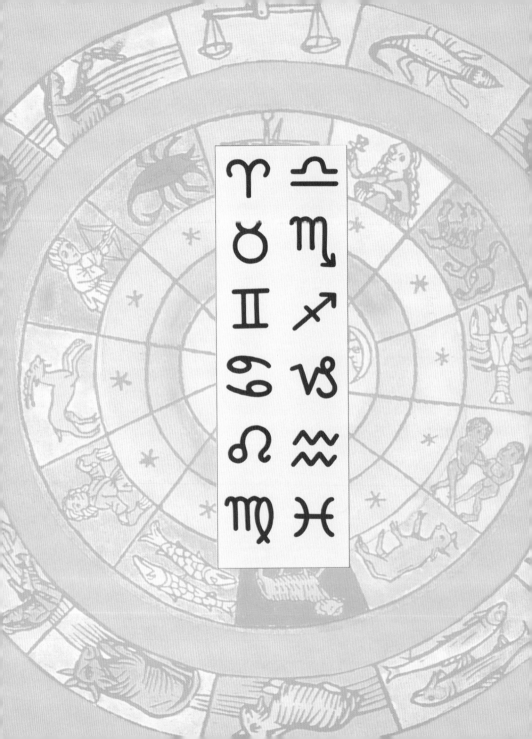

Western Astrology

At the moment of your birth, the Sun, Moon
and eight planets were at precise positions in the sky.
They were in the same segments of the sky as various
of the 12 particular constellations of stars which make up
the zodiac. The strengths and weaknesses of your personality
and some of the major events in your life
were predetermined by these astronomical positions.
This is the basis of the complex science of astrology.

Western Astrology

To most people, astrology means the highly simplified populist approach of those newspapers and magazines that feature an astrology column. This very general forecast is based solely on the stellar position of the Sun on the day of your birth and it is unlikely to have much accuracy.

Someone who says, 'I'm a Taurus', or 'I'm a Scorpio', is merely stating that the Sun was passing through the constellation of Taurus or Scorpio (respectively) when he or she was born.

This is known as 'Sun-sign astrology'. It is used because it is simple. The fact that the Sun is in the same part of the sky on a particular date every year means that, whatever your age, if you were born between 21st April and 21st May, for example, your star sign is Taurus. A twelfth of the world's population has the same Sun sign as you. Sun-sign astrology has limited accuracy.

THE ZODIAC

The zodiac is a relatively narrow band of stars (about 18° wide) against which the Sun, Moon and planets move. It stretches right around the Earth and its 360° have been divided up into 12 equal segments of 30°. These segments are named after 12 constellations of stars that more or less occupy parts of the segments.

The constellations correspond to the 12 signs of the zodiac. Note that the central line of the zodiac is known as the ecliptic.

This idea of a zodiac is very ancient – dating back as far as the time of the Babylonians, about 4,000 years ago. The Babylonians, who were relatively advanced in the studies of mathematics and astronomy developed the basis of a system of divination that studied the influence of the Sun, Moon, planets and stars.

A SHORT HISTORY OF WESTERN ASTROLOGY

It is important to remember that astrology was the same thing as astronomy for thousands of years, from Babylonian times through the refinement of techniques by the Greeks, Romans and early medieval Arabs. The early Christians, especially

St. Augustine, attacked astrology, and it was in decline in western Europe for about 800 years until the thirteenth century, when it saw some revival.

Only in the seventeenth century, when the first modern astronomers appeared, did astronomy split away

BELOW *Two fifteenth-century zodiacs, arranged concentrically.*

from astrology. At the same time, there was increased interest in astrology, especially in England, and much of the complex detail was worked out by men such as John Dee (astrologer to Queen Elizabeth I); William Lilly, who in 1648 in his Astrological Predictions forecast 'sundry fires and consuming plague' for London in about 1665 (he was correct, since the Great Plague was in 1665 and the Fire of London in 1666); Francis Moore (whose Vox Stellarum was an important early almanac, which became Old Moore's Almanac, still published each year); and Ebenezer Sibley who, in 1784, produced The Celestial Art of Astrology, the most complete and ambitious work on the subject up to that date.

Until 1931, astrological prediction had tended to be based on personal horoscopes (a horoscope is an astrological birth chart, showing the sky at the moment of birth, with the Earth in the centre surrounded by the planets and then the constellations). Essentially, they were private, produced by an astrologer for a client, and were not revealed to anybody else. But on 24 August 1931, Princess Margaret was born to the Duke and Duchess of York. (He was later King George VI; she was the late Queen Mother). The Sunday Express commissioned a birth chart of the baby and published it. This led to a sudden rekindling of interest in astrological predictions in several newspapers as a regular feature.

BELOW The Great Fire of London (1666) so successfully forecast by the astrologer William Lilly that he was actually suspected of starting the blaze.

CALCULATING A PERSONAL BIRTH CHART

It is a complex task to calculate a personal birth chart (the technical term is to erect or cast it). Only a brief outline of the procedure will be given here so that you can appreciate some of the difficulties involved.

The basic equipment needed are a pair of compasses, a pencil, a protractor, an atlas that lists latitudes and longitudes of places around the world and (the difficult part) an ephemeris, which is a book giving the positions of the Sun, Moon and planets at particular times.

Ideally, you should draw two separate discs, one of which fits around the other. The outer disc (diagram 1) needs to be divided into 30° segments inscribed with the 12 signs of the Zodiac, proceeding anticlockwise from Aries through to Pisces. The inner disc

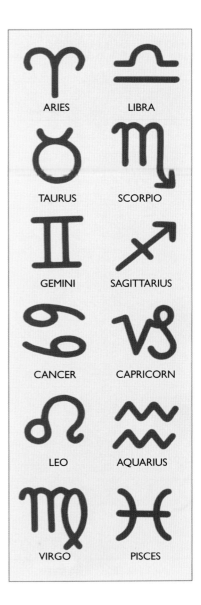

ARIES   LIBRA

TAURUS   SCORPIO

GEMINI   SAGITTARIUS

CANCER   CAPRICORN

LEO   AQUARIUS

VIRGO   PISCES

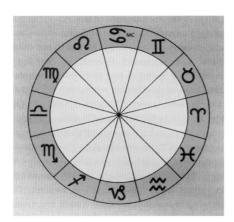

Diagram 1

25

(diagram 2) has the Earth at its centre. It is really a diagram of the sky, showing north, south, east and west, but reversed from normal maps, with east to the left. Also, it shows times, with dawn (6 A.M.) to the east (this is known as the ascendant and is very important), noon to the south (at the top of the diagram, a position also known as Medium Coeli or Midheaven), dusk to the west and midnight (Immum Coeli) to the north.

Another feature of the basic diagram is the array of houses (diagram 3). These have no astronomical significance but are important in the analysis of fortune from the chart. There are 12 houses, arranged around the inner ring, going anticlockwise from the ascendant.

The divisions between the houses and between the zodiacal signs are known as cusps. The cusp of a particular house or sign is at its starting point. So the cusp of the first house is on the ascendant. House and sign cusps will not usually coincide. Cusps are important, because a planet close to one will be affected by the houses or signs to either side of the cusp, and so any prediction needs to be amended.

To illustrate some of the difficulties of casting a birth chart, here are the time adjustments needed. If you know your time of birth to the nearest minute you must then proceed as follows:

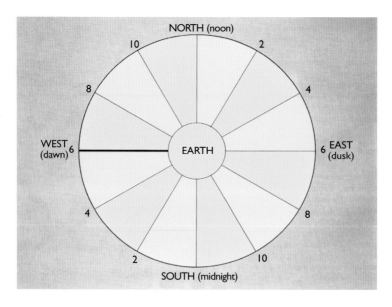

Diagram 2

Diagram 3

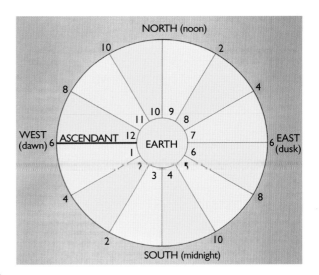

A correct your time of birth to Greenwich Mean Time (GMT) by *adding* the time difference if you were born to the west of Greenwich (if you were born in New York, add five hours), or by *subtracting* the time difference if you were born to the east of Greenwich (if you were born in Queensland, Australia, subtract ten hours). If you were born in Britain or elsewhere on the Greenwich meridian, the GMT time zone covers you and no adjustment for longitude is necessary.

B make an allowance for any daylight-saving time – that hour or occasionally more, by which some countries advance their clocks during the summer months.

C consult an ephemeris to find the sidereal time by GMT at noon on the day of your birth. Sidereal times take account of the fact that the Earth rotates on its axis in a fraction less than 24 hours. If you were born after noon, you need to add (or if before noon, subtract) a further allowance.

D having found the sidereal time of your birth, now look up the positions of the Sun, Moon and planets at that time (or adjust it from noon data). You will be able to set the ascendant on your birth chart to the correct number of degrees of the correct sign, then fasten the two separate discs together and fill in the rest of the data.

As an alternative there is now a large range of computer software available to do the job for you. All you need to do is to feed in your longitude of birth and the local time when you were born.

Houses

Each of the 12 houses is connected with a specific area of the individual's life for prediction purposes.

FIRST HOUSE

Strongly concerned with the self, this house shows how the person presents his or her personality to the world. Also connected with childhood, with development and with any new beginning. The ascending sign will always tend to dominate this house, though there is also a connection with Aries and the planet Mars. Any planet that transits this house is likely to set off some new trend in the person's life.

SECOND HOUSE

This house is connected strongly with possessions, including money, goods, property and even the prospects for earning or accumulating more money. Personal security is part of this, too. The person's capabilities (including artistic ones) are included. There are connections with Taurus and the planet Venus.

THIRD HOUSE

The subjects concerning this house pertain to communications, the relationship of the individual to the nearby environment via letters, phone calls and short journeys. Family, neighbours and acquaintances are frequently involved, though business relationships might be included. Everyday contact with others is important. The sign connected with the third house is Gemini and the planet Mercury.

FOURTH HOUSE

The home and domestic life are the subjects here, though one's original home and roots may be included. By extension, anything in this house may affect the property in which the subject lives, or the people with whom he or she lives, or even someone (like a mother) who was important during his or her formative years. The sign is Cancer and the planet is Mars.

FIFTH HOUSE

This is the 'fun' house. It is connected with leisure pursuits of all kinds – hobbies, sports, the arts, holidays – that can allow self-expression and bring happiness. Lovemaking is influenced by this house, as are pregnancy and children. ('children' can also be taken to mean one's ideas, plans and non-living creations.) The Sun and sign of Leo are associated here.

SIXTH HOUSE

This house concerns the subject's role in the community, including relationships with superiors and subordinates. Service is the keyword here, whether it is at work, in the house or elsewhere in society. Another area covered is personal health (or illness), doctors and hospitals, and also nutrition and wholesomeness. Virgo is the sign and Mercury the planet.

SEVENTH HOUSE

This is the domain of important personal relationships, especially with one's life partner, business partners and any other relationships which require co-operation. The focus is on other people and there are indications of which types the subject is best suited to (though enemies and competitors are also included). The sign is Libra and the planet Venus.

EIGHTH HOUSE

The emphasis here is on sharing, particularly money and personal possessions. So any money matters which involve others (wills, taxes, one's partners, income and assets) are included. So, too, are sexual relationships, shared feelings and any kind of beginning or ending, such as birth, death and great changes in outlook or lifestyle. The sign is Scorpio and the planet may be Pluto or Mars.

NINTH HOUSE

The expansion of horizons is covered here, literally in terms of travel to distant places or communication with them, metaphorically through further education, and spiritually through religion or philosophy. Relationships with foreigners are included, though these may just be non-blood relatives. Whatever else, a mental expansion is generally involved. The sign is Sagittarius and the planet is Jupiter.

TENTH HOUSE

The subject's career, status and goals are connected with this house. The ego is at the centre of it, and how well any ambitions are achieved or frustrated – not just in one's career but also in, for example, politics or creative pursuits. Authority figures and organizations are important here, and one's relationships with and in them. The sign connected with this house is Capricorn and the planet Saturn.

ELEVENTH HOUSE

Friendships and group activities are central in this house, though more in the realm of hobbies and pastimes than at work. There can still be hopes and ambitions involved, but these are as much for the group as for oneself. All kinds of learning (though mostly for pleasure) are included. Some unconventional or eccentric activities could be involved. Aquarius is the sign and Saturn or Uranus the planet.

TWELFTH HOUSE

This is the house concerned with solitariness – one's inner feelings, worries, psychological sufferings and doubts. It is full of negative influences, often prophesying ill health and weakness, although some positive influences, such as self-sacrifice, secret love and hidden talent are included. It is the place of illusions, day-dreams and exclusion from normal life. Pisces is the sign and Neptune or Jupiter the planet.

Planets

The seven 'planets' of the ancients were the Sun, the Moon (neither of which is actually a planet, of course), Mercury, Venus, Mars, Jupiter and Saturn, all of which were visible to the naked eye. The word planet comes from the Greek *planetes*, meaning wanderer, because to the ancients they appeared to be wandering about against the fixed backcloth of stars.

Since the invention of the telescope, the other three planets of our solar system, Uranus, Neptune and Pluto, have been discovered, although these are so distant and take so long to move through their orbits that their effect upon any astrological predictions is small.

Each of the planets has certain characteristics attached to it, which vary a little according to the zodiacal sign in which that planet was at the subject's birth or will be in the near future. These characteristics and the prospects associated with them will be modified again according to which of the houses that planet is in (or was in at the subject's birth, or is moving into during a future period which is being predicted). This kind of analysis is the stuff of which astrological prediction is made.

THE SUN

As the source of life and the 'father' of the family of planets, the Sun has the most powerful influence upon the personality. It represents self-integration, authority and vitality. It rules the heart and the spine. As a powerful 'masculine' force, it may be seen as governing the creative and generative power of man; for a woman it represents power and career prospects and also the men in her life. The good side of the Sun's influence is leadership; the bad side is arrogance and intolerance.

LEFT *The 12 signs of the zodiac from an early sixteenth-century calendar.*

The Sun influences the signs that it passes through as follows:

Aries   enterprising, enjoying control; perhaps opinionated or confrontational.

Taurus   persistent, resourceful; stubborn, a bad enemy.

Gemini   versatile, communicative; could be vague or inconsistent.

Cancer   imaginative, shrewd, home-loving; may be shy or self-pitying.

Leo   (the Sun's own sign) powerful confident, dignified; or boastful, attention-seeking.

Virgo   thoughtful, modest, efficient; may be fussy or interfering.

Libra   easy-going, diplomatic and friendly; perhaps indecisive or lazy; may lack confidence.

Scorpio   passionate, secretive, determined; may be jealous or brooding.

Sagittarius   optimistic, enthusiastic, tolerant, loving freedom; or extravagant and restless.

Capricorn   practical, serious, hard-working; may be reserved, selfish.

Aquarius   independent, idealistic; perhaps rebellious, too unconventional.

Pisces   sympathetic, kind, emotional; but impractical, secretive, timid.

THE MOON

With its 'female' qualities, the Moon represents the response to life – the moods. The Moon controls the qualities of intuition, affection and spirituality. Because the Moon is associated with water through its influence on the tides, it stands for changes, motions and rhythms, including pregnancy and the physical changes of life. Each time the Moon is full or new it has an effect on one's fortunes, and the occasional eclipses (every few months) are significant. It rules the stomach, breasts, ovaries, and digestive system. The bad features of the Moon are moodiness, impulsiveness and a tendency to excessive passivity.

The Moon and all the other planets are affected by their passage through the signs of the zodiac, as the Sun is, but this introductory guide will not list them all.

MERCURY

As the messenger of the gods in Roman mythology, it is no surprise to find that this planet's main astrological symbolism is communication. To be mercurial is to be bright, witty, volatile and physically and mentally agile; and so it is with people born under Mercury.

The head rules the heart here. Mercury is concerned with the nervous system, brain, lungs and thyroid. There is an association, too, with childhood and youth (because Mercury is the smallest of the planets), and with education. On the negative side are tendencies towards impetuousness and irrational moods; Mercury is also something of a trickster.

VENUS

This very female planet is concerned with harmony and unity. Although Venus stands for friendship and love, the connection with unbridled sexual passion is often overstated. The love of beauty, elegance, artistry and peace are Venusian traits. A man born under Venus may perhaps be controlled by a woman. The throat, kidneys and parathyroid glands are Venus's concern. The negative qualities include tendencies towards weakness, shyness and passivity in both men and women.

MARS

An active, energetic, healthy character, full of male passions. Not necessarily warlike, despite tradition, although perhaps possessing a quick temper. Other traits are fearlessness, tenacity and straightforwardness. Perhaps too aggressive and shallow. The sex glands, urinary system and kidneys are governed by Mars.

JUPITER

This, the largest of the planets, symbolizes improvement, cheerfulness, optimism, expansion and broad-mindedness. Attitudes are mature, generous and big-hearted, though moral and conservative. Affable and unselfish, seeking success but not materialistic, Jupiter represents mature middle-age. The negative side includes conceit, exaggeration, perhaps even criminal activity. It controls the body's healing, the liver and pituitary gland.

SATURN

Personified as an old man. Saturn's great strengths are responsibility and capability. The virtues of the Saturnian include caution, control, patience and thrift. It is an unhappy planet, bringing difficult circumstances, and, on its own, would be a bad influence in anybody's horoscope. There is a lack of humour, of happiness or of any real emotion. The body's skin, bones and teeth are ruled by Saturn.

URANUS

Representing change, freedom and originality, Uranus has an uncertain effect upon horoscopes. Despite its great distance from Earth, it spends seven years in each sign, and therefore it is a little more influential than might be supposed. Even so, some astrologers ignore its influence. There is a certain mysticism and willingness to behave out of character associated with Uranus subjects. Uranus controls the circulatory system and the pineal gland.

NEPTUNE

Even less significant than Uranus, due to its greater distance and slower pace, Neptune is the mystic planet, standing for intuition and the imagination. Subjects possess great sensitivity, although they tend towards vagueness, chaos and self-destroying addictions. Neptune rules not only the waves but, in the human body, the spine, parts of the nervous system and the thalamus. It is a planet that has been in only some of the constellations this century.

PLUTO

The planet of the unknown and the unconscious, Pluto stands for transformation. Its subjects are individualists. Its effects need to be faced alone. Pluto controls the reproductive system, and it is associated with beginnings and endings (birth and death). Only a few signs this century have been affected by it.

ELECTIONAL ASTROLOGY

A different approach to astrological forecasting is not to make predictions based on an existing birth date, but to select a lucky date in advance, usually used for ceremonies or starting points. Among Far Eastern societies it has been the custom to choose an auspicious day for a wedding, using planetary positions. Although such beliefs have been largely suppressed in Communist China, communities in Hong Kong, the United States, Britain and elsewhere still keep to the tradition. In fact, it is a practice that is spreading into business, with firms opening, projects beginning or contracts signed on astrologically-forecast days which will bring luck to the enterprise.

A good early example of electional astrology was when John Flamstead, Britain's first Astronomer Royal, selected the precise lucky time for founding the Greenwich observatory – at 3:14 in the afternoon of 10 August, 1675.

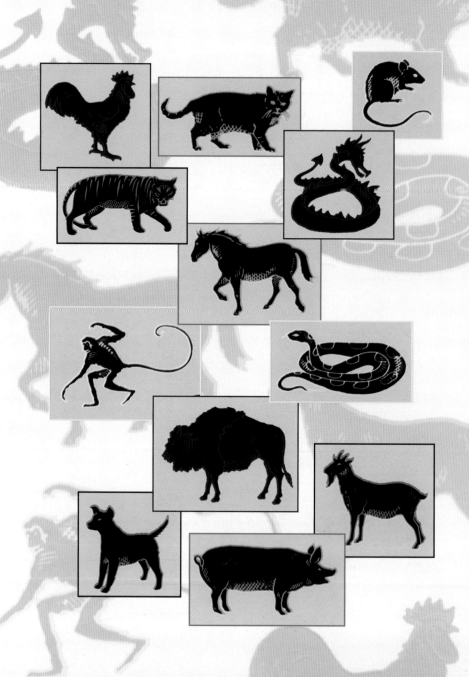

Chinese Astrology

The Chinese astrological system of animal years
has achieved such a high profile during the last few years,
with many books published on the subject and features
appearing in major magazines on the occasion of
each Chinese New Year, that there can be few
people still unaware of it.

There are 12 animal year-signs, following each other in a
regular cycle. For example, 2003 was the year of the Goat,
so was 1991, and before that 1979. The next year of the
Goat will be 2015.

The 12 animals in the cycle are (in order) the Rat, the
Buffalo or Ox, the Tiger, the Cat or Rabbit or Hare, the
Dragon, the Snake, the Horse, the Goat, the Monkey, the
Rooster or Cockerel, the Dog, and the Pig or Boar.
It is important to realize that there is no connection
between Chinese astrology and Western astrology. No
correlation exists between the 12 animals and the
12 signs of the zodiac.

The basis of the Chinese animal system is that people born in a particular year are likely to possess particular personality characteristics. So a person born in 1960 (the year of the Rat) will be different from a person born in 1959 (the year of the Pig) or 1961 (the year of the Buffalo), but will tend to have some similarities with a person born in 1948 or 1972 (also years of the Rat). This is greatly simplifying the system; in fact there are subtle differences between people born in different years carrying the same sign.

THE RAT
....

CHARACTERISTICS

Rats are often opportunists, with charm and tenacity. They are ambitious, often greedy. You will find them in company (for they tend not to be loners) but you may find them arriving late, as punctuality is not one of their strengths. Rats dislike routine work and are often to be found in jobs or professions where each day brings something new.

In love, the Rat is most compatible with other Rats and very compatible with Buffaloes, Dragons or Monkeys, but do not get on well at all with Goats or Roosters.

In marriage, the Rat should go for a Dragon, or perhaps a Goat or Pig, and certainly not a Tiger, Cat or Horse.

In business, the spouse could also be the ideal business partner, for here, too, the Dragon is the best bet.

Jan 31, 1900	to	Feb 19, 1901
Feb 18, 1912	to	Feb 6, 1913
Feb 5, 1924	to	Jan 28, 1925
Jan 24, 1936	to	Feb 11, 1937
Feb 10, 1948	to	Jan 29, 1949
Jan 28, 1960	to	Feb 15, 1961
Feb 18, 1972	to	Feb 3, 1973
Feb 2, 1984	to	Feb 20, 1985
Feb 19, 1996	to	Feb 7, 1997

FAMOUS RATS

George Bush, Joan Collins, Ivan Lendl, Prince Charles, William Shakespeare and Mozart.

THE BUFFALO

CHARACTERISTICS

Buffaloes are hard-working, strong-minded and extremely punctual. They tend not to have close friends and often suffer problems in love and marriage. Continuity is important to them, and they dislike change or interruptions. You will find them in routine jobs everywhere, in which they are often highly valued.

Feb 19, 1901	to	Feb 7, 1902
Feb 6, 1913	to	Jan 25, 1914
Jan 25, 1925	to	Feb 12, 1926
Feb 11, 1937	to	Jan 30, 1938
Jan 29, 1949	to	Feb 16, 1950
Feb 15, 1961	to	Feb 4, 1962
Feb 3, 1973	to	Jan 22, 1974
Feb 20, 1985	to	Feb 9, 1986
Feb 8, 1997	to	Jan 27, 1998

In love, the Buffalo will relate well with a Rooster or a Pig and should not attempt a relationship with a Tiger or a Goat.

In marriage, only a Rooster is really compatible, since Buffaloes are often very difficult to live with; other Buffaloes, Tigers, Dragons, Horses and Dogs are best avoided.

In business, the Buffalo gets on best with a horse or a pig and not at all with a Tiger, Dragon, Snake, Goat, Monkey or Dog.

FAMOUS BUFFALOES

Margaret Thatcher, Robert Redford, Princess Diana, Marlene Dietrich and Fidel Castro.

THE TIGER

CHARACTERISTICS

Tigers are dynamic, 'ideas' people, liable to become impatient, to quarrel, to complain loudly and to be noticed wherever they are. They can be elegant and flamboyant. Their lives are often unpredictable, with violent ups and downs. They lack endurance and often make changes just for the sake of it.

Feb 8, 1902	to	Jan 28, 1903
Jan 26, 1914	to	Feb 13, 1915
Feb 13, 1926	to	Feb 1, 1927
Jan 31, 1938	to	Feb 18, 1939
Feb 17, 1950	to	Feb 5, 1951
Feb 5, 1962	to	Jan 24, 1963
Jan 23, 1974	to	Feb 10, 1975
Feb 9, 1986	to	Jan 29, 1987
Jan 28, 1998	to	Feb 15, 1999

In love, the Tiger has great compatibility with the Dragon and only slightly less with the Horse; Buffaloes, Snakes and other Tigers are worth a Tiger's while avoiding.

In marriage, a Dog is the best partner, or perhaps a Dragon or a Pig; but a Tiger should not marry a Rat, Buffalo or Snake.

In business, the Tiger will do very well with either Dragons or Horses and should not get mixed up with Buffaloes, other Tigers, Snakes, Roosters or Dogs.

FAMOUS TIGERS

Marilyn Monroe was an archetypal Tiger. Others are Sir Alec Guinness and Queen Elizabeth II.

THE CAT
· · · · · · · · · ·

CHARACTERISTICS

Cats are sensitive and good listeners. Push them hard and you should get what you want. They like a quiet life (especially at home) and try to avoid strong emotions of any kind. A Cat is likely to be methodical in all things, light-hearted and not very deep thinkers. Cats are good to have around – they are often very popular.

Jan 29, 1903	to	Feb 15, 1904
Feb 14, 1915	to	Feb 2, 1916
Feb 2,1927	to	Jan 22, 1928
Feb 19, 1939	to	Feb 7, 1940
Feb 6, 1951	to	Feb 26, 1952
Jan 25, 1963	to	Feb 12, 1964
Feb 11,1975	to	Jan 30, 1976
Jan 29, 1987	to	Feb 28, 1988
Feb 16, 1999	to	Feb 4, 2000

In love, the Cat gets on perfectly with a Dragon, very well with a Horse, a Goat or another Cat, and fairly well with a Buffalo, a Snake, a Monkey, a Dog and a Pig; only the Rooster is incompatible.

In marriage, the Cat is easy to please, and an ideal partner for a Dragon, a Snake, a Horse or another Cat; only a Rat or a Rooster should be avoided by a Cat.

In business, the Cat has plenty of scope: is best with another Cat, highly compatible with a Rat, Dragon, Snake, Goat or Pig, and only in trouble when dealing with a Tiger or a Monkey.

FAMOUS CATS

Bob Hope, Jodie Foster, David Frost and Queen Victoria.

THE DRAGON

CHARACTERISTICS

A Dragon tends to be a showperson, somewhat flashy and arrogant, also tends to be both admired and hated, with good friends and bad enemies. Like Buffaloes they hate routine. Dragons are mostly monogamous and loyal (although they need a good partner to look after them). They are often generous and almost invariably awkward.

Feb 16, 1904	to	Feb 3, 1908
Feb 3, 1916	to	Jan 22, 1917
Jan 23, 1928	to	Feb 9, 1929
Feb 8, 1940	to	Jan 26, 1941
Feb 27, 1952	to	Feb 13, 1953
Feb 13, 1964	to	Feb 1, 1965
Jan 31, 1976	to	Feb 17, 1977
Jan 17, 1988	to	Jan 6, 1989
Feb 5, 2000	to	Jan 23, 2001

In love, the Dragon is superbly compatible with Tigers, Cats, Snakes, Horses and Monkeys and extremely good with Rats or Goats; only with Dogs or other Dragons are there likely to be serious problems.

In marriage, Dragons can similarly have great relationships with Rats, Monkeys or Roosters and pretty good ones with Tigers, Cats and Snakes; but Dragons must avoid other Dragons, Dogs and Buffaloes.

In business, Dragons do well with Rats, Tigers, Monkeys, Roosters or Pigs, but should beware of Buffaloes and Dogs.

FAMOUS DRAGONS

Jeffrey Archer, Jimmy Connors, Shirley Temple and Cliff Richard.

THE SNAKE
●●●●●●●●●●●●

CHARACTERISTICS

Snakes are wise and tenacious people, not necessarily beautiful but most often attractive. They tend towards infidelity but are also paradoxically very possessive. An artistic talent is a strong possibility, as is the ability to make money. Although preferring idleness and being prone to making wrong decisions, Snakes are good companions by virtue of their sense of humour, unwillingness to quarrel and ability to adapt to circumstances.

In love, the Snake is perfect for a Dragon, pretty good with a Horse and only incompatible with a Tiger or another Snake.

In marriage, the Snake has plenty of choice, though a Cat is best and a Tiger impossible.

In business, no relationships are perfectly smooth (they do best on their own) but they can manage with Cats.

Feb 4, 1905	to	Jan 24, 1906
Jan 23, 1917	to	Feb 10, 1918
Feb 10, 1929	to	Jan 29, 1930
Jan 27, 1941	to	Feb 14, 1942
Feb 14, 1953	to	Feb 2, 1954
Feb 21, 1965	to	Jan 20, 1966
Feb 18, 1977	to	Feb 6, 1978
Feb 6, 1989	to	Jan 27, 1990
Jan 24, 2001	to	Feb 11, 2002

FAMOUS SNAKES

Bob Dylan, Placido Domingo and Lincoln.

THE HORSE

CHARACTERISTICS

Horses are elegant, easy-going with a good sense of humour. They may possess great sex appeal. Not that the social side is all they care about – they are often hard-workers, good decision-makers and natural leaders. They love company and are excellent listeners. Their only weaknesses are falling in love too easily and making changes too frequently.

Jan 25, 1906	to	Feb 12, 1907
Feb 11, 1918	to	Jan 31, 1919
Jan 30, 1930	to	Feb 16, 1931
Feb 15, 1942	to	Feb 4, 1943
Feb 3, 1954	to	Jan 23, 1955
Jan 21, 1966	to	Feb 8, 1967
Feb 7, 1978	to	Jan 27, 1979
Jan 27, 1990	to	Feb 15, 1991
Feb 12, 2002	to	Jan 31, 2003

In love, they are superbly compatible with Goats, Dogs and other Horses, pretty good with Tigers, Cats and Snakes but should avoid Monkeys, Roosters and Pigs.

In marriage, their choice is wide, with the Cat, Goat and other Horses being best, a Rooster or Dog very good, but never a Rat, Buffalo or Monkey.

In business, a Horse should choose a Tiger or a Rooster as a business partner, though good results can be expected with a Buffalo, Cat, Dragon or Goat, but not with a Rat, a Pig or another Horse.

FAMOUS HORSES

Muhammed Ali, Clint Eastwood and Barbara Streisand.

THE GOAT
....

CHARACTERISTICS

A Goat enjoys life, but in his or her own way, preferably without restraints of any kind. Artistic and sociable. Goats are popular. They can also be fickle, insecure and bad at taking decisions. Not normally leaders, Goats are quite easily led or influenced by others.

In love, the Goat has little control and will do very well with a Horse or perhaps a Cat or a Dragon; but will not do well with a Rat, Buffalo, Rooster or Pig.

In marriage, the Horse is again best, and a Cat, Dragon or Pig can be quite compatible; Roosters and Dogs should be avoided.

In business, a Goat can get on quite well with a Cat, a Horse or a Pig, but will not get on at all with a Buffalo, a Rooster or a Dog.

Feb 13, 1907	to	Feb 1, 1908
Feb 1, 1919	to	Feb 19, 1920
Feb 17, 1931	to	Feb 5, 1932
Feb 5, 1943	to	Jan 24, 1944
Jan 24, 1955	to	Feb 11, 1956
Feb 9, 1967	to	Jan 29, 1968
Jan 28, 1979	to	Feb 15, 1980
Jan 17, 1988	to	Jan 6, 1989
Feb 16, 1991	to	Feb 3, 1992
Feb 1, 2003	to	Jan 21, 2004

FAMOUS GOATS

Mikhail Gorbachev, Andy Warhol, John Major, Mick Jagger and Michelangelo.

THE MONKEY
• • • • • • • • • • • • • •

CHARACTERISTICS

The Monkey is a tricky person, quick, opportunistic and often good with numbers. He or she knows it, too, and is not modest. Monkeys have excellent memories and possess the potential to be very successful. Not succeeding would be due to impatience, superficiality and inability to share. At the same time, Monkeys can be generous and thoughtful people.

Feb 2, 1908	to	Jan 21, 1909
Feb 20, 1920	to	Feb 7, 1921
Feb 6, 1932	to	Jan 25, 1933
Jan 25, 1944	to	Feb 12, 1945
Feb 12, 1956	to	Jan 30, 1957
Jan 30, 1968	to	Feb 16, 1969
Feb 16, 1980	to	Feb 4, 1981
Feb 4, 1992	to	Jan 23, 1993
Jan 22, 2004	to	Feb 8, 2005

In love, the Monkey is highly compatible with Dragons, Pigs and other Monkeys, compatible with Rats and completely at odds with both both Horses and Dogs.

In marriage, it is very similar, with Dragons, Pigs and other Monkeys making ideal mates, Goats making good ones and Horses or Roosters being the worst.

In business, the Monkey can work well in partnership with a Dragon or a Pig and not at all with a Buffalo, Cat, Rooster or Dog.

FAMOUS MONKEYS

Michael Douglas, Elizabeth Taylor, Sebastian Coe, Ian Fleming and Diana Ross.

THE ROOSTER

CHARACTERISTICS

An honest and generous person, the Rooster offers you free advice whether you want it or not (though some Roosters are less extrovert). They can be either miserly or rash spenders. Almost always they are efficient, methodical people, though perhaps lacking in initiative.

Jan 22, 1909	to	Feb 9, 1910
Feb 8, 1921	to	Jan 27, 1922
Jan 26, 1933	to	Feb 13, 1934
Feb 13, 1945	to	Feb 1, 1946
Jan 31, 1957	to	Feb 17, 1958
Feb 17, 1969	to	Feb 5, 1970
Feb 5, 1981	to	Jan 24, 1982
Jan 23, 1993	to	Feb 10, 1994
Feb 9, 2005	to	Jan 28, 2006

In love, only the Buffalo is compatible, since Roosters are really interested in more permanent relationships.

In marriage, the Dragon is ideal, the Buffalo, Snake or Horse almost as good, while the Cat, Goat, Monkey or another Rooster are just impossible to live with.

In business, the Rooster gets on well with Dragons and Horses, slightly with Buffaloes and hardly at all with anyone else.

FAMOUS ROOSTERS

Nick Faldo, Gloria Estefan, Eric Clapton and Errol Flynn.

THE DOG

CHARACTERISTICS

Dogs are hard-working people, loyal friends and can be great opponents of injustice. They may be stubborn or get bogged down with small details, and they do best as followers, not leaders. They have very high standards by which they judge themselves and those around them. They can be pessimistic.

In love, the Dog is wonderfully suited to a Horse or a Pig and not at all compatible with a Dragon or a Goat.

In marriage, a Tiger or a Pig is ideal; a Buffalo, Dragon or Goat is best avoided.

In business, only the Pig will make a good partner; most other partnerships will not work.

Feb 10, 1910	to	Jan 29, 1911
Jan 28, 1922	to	Feb 15, 1923
Feb 4, 1934	to	Jan 23, 1935
Feb 2, 1946	to	Jan 21, 1947
Feb 18, 1958	to	Feb 7, 1959
Feb 6, 1970	to	Jan 26, 1971
Jan 25, 1982	to	Feb 12, 1983
Feb 10, 1994	to	Jan 31, 1995
Jan 29, 2006	to	Feb 17, 2007

FAMOUS DOGS

Madonna, Uri Geller, Liza Minelli, Winston Churchill and Michael Jackson.

THE PIG

CHARACTERISTICS

Pigs are very hard workers and can be great moneymakers, especially as part of a team. They are open, straight-forward people, strong-minded and self-confident without being cocky. Their generosity and steadfastness make them excellent friends. They can fall in love easily and take rejection very badly.

In love, the Pig is pretty compatible with anyone except a Horse, though especially suited to a Dog or another Pig.

In marriage, it's even better, ideal partners being Monkeys, Dogs or other Pigs, no signs being ruled out.

In business, the Pig does best with a Monkey or a Dragon, and should avoid Horses.

Jan 30, 1911	to	Feb 17, 1912
Feb 16, 1923	to	Feb 4, 1924
Feb 4, 1935	to	Jan 23, 1936
Jan 22, 1947	to	Feb 9, 1948
Feb 8, 1959	to	Jan 27, 1960
Jan 27, 1971	to	Jan 15, 1972
Feb 13, 1983	to	Feb 1, 1984
Jan 31, 1995	to	Feb 19, 1996
Feb 18, 2007	to	Feb 6, 2008

FAMOUS PIGS

Woody Allen, Elton John and Maria Callas.

Signs of the Zodiac

There are various ways of classifying the 12 zodiac signs, and these help us to understand the fundamental nature of each sign – the things that they have in common and how they differ.

More about The 12 Signs

Each of the 12 zodiac signs belongs to both an element and mode group. By studying these, we can learn for example, that Aries is a Cardinal Fire sign, combining the elemental qualities of enthusiasm and assertion with the mode qualities of initiation and action. You can easily work out the combination for your own Sun sign and those of family and friends.

ELEMENTS

The 12 signs are divided into four elements: Fire, Air, Water and Earth. Each element has three signs within its group, and because of this, they are also named the triplicities, meaning groups of three.

Fire and Air are known as the positive or masculine elements, representing energy rising upwards and extroversion. The **Fire signs** are Aries, Leo and Sagittarius. Fire signs are enthusiastic, self-confident, assertive, courageous and usually display a great love of life. The **Air signs** are Gemini, Libra and Aquarius. Air is spacious and free-moving symbolizing thought and intellect. These signs love thinking, and can be quite analytical and detached, but they also need to communicate.

The feminine and negative elements are Water and Earth. They tend towards introversion, and represent energy moving downwards. The **Earth signs** are Taurus, Virgo and Capricorn. These signs are very down-to-earth, solid, practical and concerned with the material world. The three **Water signs** are Cancer, Scorpio and Pisces. Water signs are in tune with their emotions, and usually have powerful imaginations and feelings.

A strong affinity exists between signs of each element group because they share many of the same characteristics. The six positive signs will have much in common, as will the six negative.

Another way to classify the signs is by their mode, or their quality of operating. The modes describe how a sign takes action and its phase of manifestation. There are three modes, each with four signs. These groupings are also termed the quadruplicities. The first mode is named 'Cardinal', or fundamental, and this group consists of Aries, Cancer, Libra and Capricorn. Cardinal signs are good at initiating and taking action. They represent the four seasonal equinox points, with Aries beginning on the 21st of March,

Cancer on the 21st of June, and so on.

The second mode is 'Fixed'. The Fixed signs are Taurus, Leo, Scorpio and Aquarius. Fixed signs are drawn towards keeping things stable and enduring. When the Sun is in the Fixed signs, each season comes to its peak.

The last mode is 'Mutable', which means changeable and adaptable. The Mutable signs are Gemini, Virgo, Sagittarius and Pisces. These four signs are highly adaptable and quick to change or move on. They are found at the end of each season, when nature is in transition.

ABOVE *This fourteenth-century picture shows the Cardinal sign of Aries has always had a reputation for action, energy and plenty of physical activity!*

BELOW *This chart shows the 12 signs with their elements, modes and types. It is interesting to note that people of masculine signs tend to be extroverts and those of feminine signs to be introverts.*

Sign	Symbol	Element	Mode	Type
Aries	♈	Fire	Cardinal	Masculine
Taurus	♉	Earth	Fixed	Feminine
Gemini	♊	Air	Mutable	Masculine
Cancer	♋	Water	Cardinal	Feminine
Leo	♌	Fire	Fixed	Masculine
Virgo	♍	Earth	Mutable	Feminine
Libra	♎	Air	Cardinal	Masculine
Scorpio	♏	Water	Fixed	Feminine
Sagittarius	♐	Fire	Mutable	Masculine
Capricorn	♑	Earth	Cardinal	Feminine
Aquarius	♒	Air	Fixed	Masculine
Pisces	♓	Water	Mutable	Feminine

SUN AND PLANETS

Each sign is associated with one or two planets in particular, which are then said to rule the sign. These rulerships show similarities between certain planets and signs, and help astrologers to understand the meaning of both.

The **Sun** shows your basic spirit and vitality, your type of power and how you grow as an individual. Much of your creative drive is symbolized by your Sun sign, and the Sun is always one of the most important factors in any chart, representing your fundamental consciousness and how you express your will. The Sun in a woman's chart is one of the indications of what sort of man she will be attracted to. The Sun rules the sign of Leo.

The **Moon** represents your instincts and basic emotional responses, giving information about your subconscious and unconscious mind, and how you react defensively. In a somewhat overly male-dominated modern world, the Moon is a vital indicator of the feminine side of your nature and is linked to childbirth. It also represents what sort of environment you feel comfortable in, and for a man, the Moon often reveals the type of woman he is drawn towards. The Moon rules the sign of Cancer.

Mercury reveals how you think and communicate – how your mind works, what you think about and your ability to make decisions. It can symbolize intelligence. Mercury is a planet that is never more than one sign away from the Sun. This means that your Mercury will be placed either in the same sign as your Sun, or the one preceeding or following it. Thus, if your sign is Cancer, your Mercury sign will be either Gemini, Cancer or Leo. Therefore, the position of Mercury can strongly modify the influence of your Sun sign. For example, an Aries with Mercury in sensitive Pisces will be much more reflective and emotional than a typical Arien. Mercury rules the signs of Gemini and Virgo

ABOVE *A French zodiac, revealing the link between the signs and the various parts of the body. This concept was widely used in medical astrology.*

Venus represents how you relate to others and your image of love. It describes your behaviour in relationships, as well as your social values and attitudes. It is also one of the planets that relates to finances. The placement of Venus in a man's chart depicts his image of an ideal mate. Venus rules the signs of Taurus and Libra.

Mars symbolizes your sexuality and energy. It also shows how you take action and initiate the impulsive desires you may have, and the ambitions arising from these. Mars represents your fighting spirit, or how you stand up for yourself. For a woman, the placement of Mars in her chart describes her image of an ideal man. Mars rules Aries, and also shares rulership of Scorpio with Pluto.

Jupiter represents your sense of expansion and opprtunity. It shows your good fortune and luck in life, and how you are enabled to be positive. A strongly placed Jupiter can help you find much joy, happiness and optimism. Jupiter rules Sagittaarius, and also shares rulership of Pisces with Neptune.

Saturn displays your level of discipline, and how you deal with restriction and delays. It concerns authority, hard work and the handling of responsibility, and has therefore been called 'the taskmaster'. Saturn has sole rulership of Capricorn, and is a joint ruler with Uranus of Aquarius. In olden days, Saturn signified the extent of the known solar system and because of this became linked with limitation but also with qualities of persistence and tenacity.

Since the outer three planets move very slowly through the heavens, they reveal generational themes as well as individual characteristics. For example, the generation of people born around the 1960s (all those born between September 1957 and September 1971), when Pluto was in the sign of Virgo, would share a concern for ecology and the environment suggested by this astrological placement.

Uranus represents your urge for freedom and individuality. It can also show how you rebel against authority and why. Uranus is often featured in science fiction and the exploration of space. It is usually asscociated with originality, independence and occasionally with rebellion and perversity.

Neptune is concerned with your sense of yearning, ideals and desire to merge with something greater than yourself. It reveals how you seek to escape from the trials and tribulations of life.

Finally, **Pluto** signifies how you regenerate and transform yourself. It also covers taboos and that which is deeply hidden such as buried feelings and emotions.

Aries

Like your namesake, the Ram, you are a natural leader. Born
at the beginning of the zodiac, you are used to being first and
possess a pioneering, determined spirit.
Your abundant physical and mental energy helps you to make your
mark on the world. For some Ariens this may be through sport;
for others, work provides the necessary challenges – but whatever the
field, all Ariens need outside activities in which to assert themselves,
and seek action, daring and adventure.

You are at heart fearless, and this openness to meet life head-on is one of your greatest assets.

However it can also be your undoing, as you tend to rush in where angels fear to tread. Impulsive and gutsy, your initial reactions and decisions usually turn out well, but with age comes wisdom, which allows you to hold back when necessary

As the infant of the zodiac, you are concerned with yourself, and sometimes selfishly ignore the feelings of others, although they do admire the energy and enthusiasm you show in whatever you do.

Most Ariens are driven by a need to win, and this gives you a very competitive attitude. You simply must come first, and want to make sure that everyone else knows it. Because of this, you thrive on rivalry, which is fine as long as you can sometimes accept second place. You are not Superman – even though you try to be!

Hungry for new experiences, your great sense of humour helps you to get the most out of life. Unfortunately, you become bored and restless quite easily Perseverance is a trait that most Ariens have to work on – it's all very well having so many brilliant ideas, but without focus and discipline, nothing actually happens. Once you find out what you really want to do, nothing can stop you from achieving your goals.

In appearance, the males of the sign are tall and lean, with a good bone structure and strong physical presence. You are energetic and walk with a quick, confident gait, taking long strides as you move. You may have a scar or mark on your head, often from a previous fight or adventure.

You are a very physical person; which will almost certainly manifest itself in some sort of sporting activity. Because you are so in touch with your body and enjoy it, you fear physical disability more than most people.

Straightforward and direct, you throw yourself into life without thinking too much about the consequences. You enjoy taking the initiative, and won't be too happy having to follow others for long periods of time. You love simplicity

ABOVE *You are drawn by extreme challenges, and the lure of mountain climbing offers you the chance to pit your wits against the might of nature.*

EXERCISE

Regular and vigorous exercise is very important to the typical Arien. Sports offer the perfect outlets to channel your abundant physical energy. Many Ariens are drawn to the martial arts, as these provide the sort of demanding challenge you like. Fast and energetic pursuits, such as running and cycling, are also popular. Your desire for adventure and excitement can lead you to take an interest in risky activities such as mountain climbing and motor racing. You want to compete, so whichever sport you choose, you will enter it with enthusiasm, determined to be the best in the shortest possible time.

and try to set clear goals, even on a day-to-day basis. The past does not hold back a typical Aries – however many times life knocks you down, you are able to pick yourself up and try again as your confidence is virtually in-exhaustible, and so is your desire to prove yourself and get what you want.

Although independent and very much a 'man's man' you gain tremendously from being in a loving relationship, as your blunt nature benefits from a woman's sensitivity.

Most Arien women are slim, as your active lifestyle doesn't allow you any time to get fat! Your body is usually lithe, and gives an impression of tremendous vitality. Like Arien males, you walk at a fast pace—often one or two steps ahead of your friends. You are a bit of a tomboy, and this will be reflected in your dress.

You have a very talkative nature and, unlike many, are not afraid to assert yourself. This forthright manner can get you into trouble, and you are sometimes taken aback by the reactions you get.

ABOVE *Aries, from an English Psalter, York, c.1170*

PRESENTS

- Personalized gifts
- Hats and sportswear
- Surprises
- Tools
- Car accessories
- Books related to current interests
- Cash
- Weekend breaks
- Spicy meals
- Lessons for adventure sports

You are very idealistic, and will stick up for the underdog. If you are committed to a cause, you are prepared to fight with every ounce of your strength. You are one of life's optimists, and believe that you can achieve the impossible. Although you are undeniably feminine, you relate well to men, and often prefer their company. You are very independent, and are quite happy to live on your own. Arien women have a reputation for being emotionally tough, but secretly you desire a man who is strong enough to share your dreams.

For most Ariens, one of the most important considerations when choosing clothes is comfort. Yours is such a physical sign that you avoid garments that restrict movement; even for work, comfort is a must. Ariens love simplicity. and once you have found combinations that work well, tend to stick to them. Although you favour fairly conventional styles, if you want to wear something you will, regardless of what anyone else thinks.

For casual attire, sports clothes are a popular choice for both sexes. You love to feel physically free, and your natural presence gives you a vibrant and healthy look. For work clothes, you are attracted to outfits that are simple, stylish and unfussy Ariens are impatient, and you like to be able to change clothes quickly. Red is a favourite colour and adds a dynamic splash that really suits your personality. Arien women may prefer to wear trousers a lot of the time, because you could feel a bit uncomfortable in a skirt or dress You might also be reluctant to use too much make-up.

When dressing up, male Ariens look good in formal outfits which reflect their athletic physique. You certainly like to look manly! For women, a special

HEALTH

The average Aries is favoured with an extremely strong constitution, which means that you will shrug off most minor complaints with ease. Your busy workload is liable to make you overdo it physically, and this is when problems can occur. Aries rules the head, and many of you suffer from headaches and migraines, especially when under stress.

Your fiery nature also makes you prone to fevers, but these will generally be intense and short-lived. If you become ill, you tend to rush back on your feet and sometimes prolong recovery by doing so before you are ready.

Your active lifestyle makes you vulnerable to accidents, particularly when tired and run down. Living at a fast pace can mean skipping main meals and snacking on junk food, which causes problems with your digestion. Make sure you have a healthy, balanced diet, with plenty of fresh produce – you need the best possible fuel for your body. When young, you may take your robust health for granted, but as the years progress, it becomes apparent that you are not indestructible. For Ariens, a little foresight has its benefits.

defined. You prefer clear and direct interior designs, with bold colour schemes that don't take long to paint. You like to create a bright, fresh atmosphere, and will often sleep with the window open, even in the middle of winter.

Because you are so physically active and like doing things yourself, many Ariens are very practical, and do their own home and car maintenance. Although you will probably have green fingers, gardening is not something that usually appeals. If it does, you like plants that grow as fast as possible.

Your competitive nature means that your home is often a showcase for your success in life. As you progress in your career, you will happily invest in your home to reflect your increasing status. Although you are friendly towards your neighbours, you won't put up with any annoying behaviour from them. Many Ariens have such a busy lifestyle that your home will often function simply as a place that you visit occasionally.

Most Ariens have a real ability for making money. However, your impulsive and active nature can find it hard to hold onto it! Because you live on a day-to-day basis, taking a long-term view is hard. A life insurance plan is unlikely to appeal when you are young. Some

occasion is an opportunity to look better than everyone else, and you love to win attention with a stylish and sexy image, which will probably involve a new outfit and the latest perfume.

The Arien need for space and simplicity means that your home is usually uncluttered. You like to feel that you can move around from room to room unhindered, and whatever furniture there is tends to be simple and well

Ariens like money for the freedom it offers, and others like it for the power it brings. You can be generous, but you will always look after number one.

If you are not earning enough cash from your work, you quickly seek other avenues. Second jobs or starting your own business are popular choices. You are extremely creative, and it's relatively easy for most Ariens to begin a business project. The question is, will it last? You get so bored and restless that many good ideas go to waste. However, for an Aries, the rewards of being your own boss are so great that many of you manage to overcome your initial impatience.

When it comes to investment, avoid get-rich-quick schemes. Most Ariens learn the hard way and, after a few false starts, you eventually realize success can't be forced. Maintaining regular savings becomes enjoyable after initial funds have been built up.

As well as sports, many Ariens love games. Your desire to win gives you the necessary motivation to practice and persist. Aries being the most active sign, you prefer to spend your leisure time doing something. Lazing around and taking it easy just isn't you. Most Ariens love driving for pleasure, and will often go for a drive to unwind. You like going fast and can be reckless, so you have more near-accidents than others. Books and films have to be fast-paced to hold your

	How Aries finds:		At a glance
♈ Aries	Aries	Unstable fireworks	❤❤❤
♉ Taurus	Taurus	Dull and Predictable	❤
♊ Gemini	Gemini	Stimulating fun	❤❤❤❤
♋ Cancer	Cancer	Too emotional	❤❤
♌ Leo	Leo	Strong, passionate love	❤❤❤❤
♍ Virgo	Virgo	No understanding	❤
♎ Libra	Libra	Winning partnership	❤❤❤❤❤
♏ Scorpio	Scorpio	Good as an affair	❤❤❤
♐ Sagittarius	Sagittarius	Fire sign perfection	❤❤❤❤❤
♑ Capricorn	Capricorn	Don't bother	❤❤
♒ Aquarius	Aquarius	A laid-back combo	❤❤❤❤
♓ Pisces	Pisces	Unfocused	❤❤

TRADITIONAL ASSOCIATIONS

Colours:
Red, white mixed with red

Countries:
Poland, Germany, England

Tarot Card:
Number 4, the Emperor

Flowers:
Tiger Lily

Birthstone:
Ruby, diamond

Animals:
Ram, tiger, dragon

Occupations:
Firefighters, Police, Psychiatrists, Business executives

Herbs:
Nettles

Trees:
Thorn, chestnut, holly

Cities:
Krakow, Florence, Brunswick, Naples

Food:
Garlic, onions, leeks, spicy foods

RIGHT A firefighter tackles a fierce blaze, displaying the Arien qualities of bravery and cool nerves in the heat of the moment.

interest.

You eat out quite a lot, and enjoy spending time with friends. You are adventurous when eating, and hot, spicy food is especially popular. You love to party, and periodically you burn the candle at both ends.

The typical Aries adores travel, and you will have as many vacations as your budget allows. Your need for adventure is fulfiled by exploring other cultures, and you are quite happy to rough it, as long as you have plenty of excitement.

Standing around waiting is liable to make you irritable; time is of the essence and should not be wasted. You prefer shopping to meet your needs as they arise. Having to plan carefully for the future can be very constricting for you.

You have strong principles, and feel actions speak louder than words. Ariens dislike cowardly behaviour, and you will go out of your way to confront problems head-on. You find that your energy wanes when life gets too complicated. In general, clarity and purpose make an Aries happy.

Taurus

If you were born under the Sun sign of Taurus, you are strong willed with a very down-to-earth attitude towards life in general. You have a real need for security and will feel unsettled unless you are comfortable on both a material and emotional level.

Taureans like to have every aspect of their world running in a regular rhythm, and are instinctively in tune with natural cycles. Your easy-going and earthy nature gives you great potential for happiness.

Taureans have a gentle manner, which sometimes belies your determination to achieve your goals. If you feel something is worthwhile, then you are prepared to wait, no matter how long it takes. Taureans are probably the most patient sign of the zodiac!

Because money is important to you, a lot of your energy will be spent making sure that you are financially secure. Taureans work extremely hard in their pursuit of wealth. You are interested in material things, and possessions of all kinds appeal to you.

Whatever it is that you are buying, quality is a prime concern. Most Taureans avoid cheaply made, inferior goods, and would rather spend more to get something of lasting value. Sometimes you take this materialistic outlook to extremes, obtaining all your emotional security from money and possessions. This can hinder the way you relate to others, and should therefore be kept in check.

Your requirements from life are generally very basic; as well as material success, a solid relationship is very important. Taureans are very physical, and enjoy life to the fullest. A secure home and fulfiling job, good food and wine, and someone to share it with you go a long way towards making you happy. Taureans are well-adapted to living in the world, and unlike some other signs, derive real and lasting satisfaction from the simple things in life.

The typical Taurus male has a somewhat stocky appearance, with a noticeably thick neck. You have naturally well-developed muscles, and this solid physical presence will show itself no matter how much clothing you are wearing. As you walk you take slow, deliberate steps, your large feet connecting well with the ground

Solid, dependable, and practical, you like to know where you stand in the world. Taureans take a long-term view perspective. Your career is extremely important, as it provides the material platform for success in other areas of your life. Once you have your mind set on achieving something, nothing will distract you from reaching your goal.

Taureans are essentially placid, but you can react with surprising strength of purpose when pushed. You don't lose your temper easily, but when you do, others had better watch out!

ABOVE *You have a sure touch when it comes to handling money, but try not to get too carried away with the pursuit of wealth.*

EXERCISE

Unless they absolutely have to, most Taureans avoid strenuous exercise. Attempts to keep your weight down may find you working out in the gym, but otherwise you prefer going for a walk or gardening. Motivation will be increased if you live in the country.

Taurean women often have an interest in dancing and yoga, especially when they realize how much their figure benefits from stretching. Male Taureans sometimes like to use their natural physical prowess in wrestling and boxing, although most of you would rather be a spectator!

You have strong opinions and cling to these quite tenaciously, even when they work against you. Taureans are also averse to change, and you sometimes miss great opportunities because of this.

Having a partner is necessary for you to feel complete as a man, although you do need to feel financially secure before getting married and setting up a home.

Taurean women are very sensual. They tend to have full, rounded figures that convey a healthy, physical look, rosy cheeks and beautiful, lustrous hair. Like the men, you walk with slow, solid strides, which give an impression of being in touch with the ground.

You have a strong sense of right and wrong, and can be very uncompromising in living up to your own standards. Taurus is a very moral sign, displaying real courage in following principles. Being so practical in most areas of life, your head will usually rule your heart. You are romantic, but your material needs are also very strong, and you simply won't be happy or at peace unless these criteria are satisfied.

You have a commonsense approach to life, and dislike fussy, complicated situations. Taureans are very grounded, and are therefore good in a crisis. It takes a lot to truly unnerve you. You are physically tough, and able to work for long periods without rest. You enjoy earthly pleasures, and have no trouble indulging your deep sensuality. Colours and textures are very important to you, and you greatly appreciate the finer things in life. Although you can easily live on your own, a stable relationship with someone you trust gives you the security you need in order to really blossom.

PRESENTS

- Quality gifts with lasting value
- Fresh flowers, with lovely scents
- Plants for the garden
- Books on finance
- Perfumes in attractive bottles
- Luxurious beauty creams
- CDs or tapes
- Stocks and shares
- Dinner at a fine restaurant
- Fine wines or champagne

LEFT *A favourite Taurean occupation – relaxing and enjoying a luxurious lifestyle!*

Both sexes tend to dress conventionally – you don't like presenting an image that is too unusual. Taureans view clothes as an investment, and are happy to spend hard-earned cash on classic, quality items that will last, as your self-worth is enhanced by having expensive outfits that look and feel good.

Most Taureans prefer natural fabrics, and will avoid synthetics wherever possible. As a result, cottons and silks are real favourites. Most Taurean women love floral patterns, and generally seek work and casual clothes with a rich, sensuous appeal. You love the feeling of luxury next to your skin! You also like rich beauty creams and perfumes of all sorts, especially those with strong aromas.

Male Taureans prefer traditional styles, and are very comfortable in a suit. If you have the funds, it will be expertly tailored, as you regard it as a worthwhile investment.

All Taureans choose office wear that is smart, functional, and classy. Making the right impression both socially and at work is important; although you appreciate clothes in their own right, you also like to show that you can

HEALTH

Many Taureans have difficulties with their weight. You love good food and wine, and this is often consumed in large quantities. But your metabolism can be sluggish, and your easy-going manner does little to burn off all those calories. In later years, it may be necessary to watch what you eat, but most Taureans have a very resilient constitution which can carry extra pounds. When you do become ill, you are able to fight with tremendous strength and determination, often recovering through willpower alone.

The parts of the body related to Taurus are the neck and throat, and this is one area where health problems can occur. Infections range from mild sore throats to laryngitis and swollen glands.

You are also prone to stiff necks, which are usually the result of tension that has accumulated over a period of time. You like to stay calm, and as a result, can sometimes repress feelings of anger and stress. Taureans gain much from letting off steam through some sort of physical activity – a sure-fire way to combat the debilitating effects of your sometimes all-too-sedentary lifestyle.

RIGHT *This Taurus subject, from a sixteenth-century Turkish treatise exhibits the love of music of some born under the sign by the lyre he is carrying*

afford the best labels. Dressing up gives you a chance to bring out the finest outfits in your wardrobe.

For more casual attire, simple, natural designs are favoured. You want to feel comfortable and relaxed, and often enjoy hanging around in jeans and a T-shirt.

A secure, comfortable home is very important to a Taurean's sense of well-being. You like big, solid, traditional buildings that look like they were built to last. As soon as you are able, you invest in an apartment or house, and take great pleasure from owning your own home.

Many Taureans have a natural affinity for the country, and if you can't actually live there, you will do your best to have a garden. If this isn't possible, you will still seek to put your green fingers to good use, at the very least having one or two houseplants.

You love chunky furniture made out of natural materials such as wood and leather. Substantial pine tables, sumptuous beds and luxurious leather sofas are items found in many Taurean homes. Gradually you will fill your house with valuable objects, and appliances, such as a washing machine and refrigerator, will be the best you can afford.

When it comes to interior designs, you like pastel shades, and enjoy painting and selecting attractive fabrics for curtains and rugs. Floral prints are a common theme, and these are often complemented with flowers, preferably from your own garden!

Money matters are extremely important to Taureans. At an early age, you are aware of its effect on your sense of security. Many Taurus children keep full piggy banks!

You have one of the most astute financial brains of the zodiac, and find it easy to balance the books. You like dealing with money, which is why, for so many Taureans, investment becomes an enjoyable and profitable hobby.

Your methodical and pragmatic approach shows itself in the sort of investments you choose. Long-term viability is a priority, since you want to make sure that you and your loved ones are financially secure in the years to come. You are a natural with the stock market, and select safe stocks that you have researched beforehand.

If you have the funds, you like to express your artistic side, and will buy art and antiques that not only look good but will eventually increase in value. Many Taureans become quite wealthy at some point. However, rather than just hoarding money for its own sake, you also like using it to get the maximum enjoyment out of life. Friends and family around you certainly benefit from your generosity.

Taureans know how to enjoy life, and make the most of any leisure time. Resting and taking it easy is something that comes naturally, and you like to relax by watching TV, reading and listening to your favourite music. Sometimes Taureans are prone to periods of laziness, and find it hard to motivate themselves. Going out to dinner with friends is something you like to do as often as you can. Taureans make good cooks, but you

	How Taurus finds:		At a glance
♈	Aries	Too fiery	❤❤
♉	Taurus	All or nothing	❤❤❤❤❤
♊	Gemini	Flighty	❤
♋	Cancer	Deep love	❤❤❤❤
♌	Leo	Once in a while	❤❤❤
♍	Virgo	Earth sign delight	❤❤❤❤❤
♎	Libra	Possible	❤❤❤
♏	Scorpio	Opposites attract	❤❤❤❤
♐	Sagittarius	No way!	❤
♑	Capricorn	Seriously good	❤❤❤❤❤
♒	Aquarius	Mismatch	❤❤❤
♓	Pisces	Sweet and loving	❤❤❤❤

certainly appreciate the luxury of having someone else do all the work.

Taureans are well-known for their love of gardening: caring for plants gives you a profound sense of satisfaction. You are also passionate about music, and can have a talent for singing. At the very least, you will own a good sound system.

Your taste ranges from classical, particularly opera, to the more thumping sounds of modern music. Being artistic, Taureans are also drawn to painting and pottery. You love working with the sensuous textures of paints and clay.

Taureans like routines, and adjusting to change can be difficult. You love pleasure, and will repeat the same experiences, enjoying each time as much as the last. You are not one for huge surprises, although a thoughtful gift is welcome. Taureans like to go at their own pace, and you resent people who hurry you.

Poverty is upsetting for most Taureans, and a healthy bank balance helps you to sleep soundly.

TRADITIONAL ASSOCIATIONS

Colours:
Green and pink

Countries:
Iran, Ireland, Cyprus

Tarot Card:
Number 5, the Pope

Flowers:
Rose

Birthstone:
Emerald, topaz

Animals:
Bull, elephant

Occupations:
Farmers, Florists, Bankers, Beauty therapists

Herbs:
Mint

Trees:
Almond, apple, plum

Cities:
Dublin, Leipzig St. Louis

Food:
Potatoes, chocolate

LEFT *Taureans love being with nature and also have a need to feel secure. So for many of you, a large, comfortable house in the country really would be an ideal home.*

Gemini

Geminis are highly restless, and your active brains need almost constant mental stimulation. This means that in virtually all areas of your life, you seek a wide variety of contrasting experiences. Boredom is to be avoided at all costs!

Curious and alert, you love communicating with others, and never run out of things to talk about. Your versatile mind picks up facts quickly, and you love acquiring knowledge. So many topics interest you that there is a danger of only gaining a rather superficial understanding of several subjects. It is difficult for a Geminian to concentrate on anything for a long period of time, and this is one reason why many of you find it hard to maintain a consistent lifestyle.

Gemini is a complex sign; the twins represent the inherent duality of your nature. Your two halves need contrasts, and you feel uncomfortable without them. You thrive on nervous energy and love being busy. Geminis will typically read more than one book at the same time, hold down two or three jobs, study something new at night school and still have energy for a hectic social schedule, which may or may not include a partner.

On a deep level, this fragmentation is a reflection of your search to integrate your many selves. As you get older you discover one or two things that you really want to focus on, and these bring much happiness and contentment.

You will always retain a youthfulness that enables you to look at the world with fresh eyes. Sometimes called the Peter Pan of the zodiac, you relate well to children; preferring to stay childlike yourself, you avoid heavy commitments. Geminians never stop learning, and provided you find constructive outlets for your immense mental energy, life will always be rewarding and full of interest.

The Gemini male is normally tall and lean, and he walks at a brisk pace, looking around as he goes. You are agile, and your eyes convey the curiosity for which your sign is famous. Geminians age slowly, and generally appear much younger than their years.

For many Gemini men, life is one big adventure, and you find it hard to resist any new experience. Ever curious, your need for stimulation takes you down some fascinating roads, and you often end up flirting with danger. You want to taste so much of life that it's just as well that you are clever and persuasive, as you are able to use your charm to great advantage. You are intelligent and witty, and need positive mental challenges to stop you from getting bored.

You are unlikely to settle down for some time, as you feel there are too many things you want to do before making commitments.

ABOVE *For many Geminians, a game of tennis is the perfect way to relax and have fun.*

EXERCISE

Geminians usually live off their nerves, and can neglect their health. You gain much from regular physical exercise. It helps you to stay relaxed, and puts you in touch with your body. You enjoy tennis and squash, and prefer exercising in a social environment – joining a health club and working out with others is a lot more fun.

You are mentally active, and sometimes it can be hard for you to switch off. Meditation and gentle forms of Eastern movement, such as yoga and t'ai chi, offer a way to help you to unwind and discover serenity.

As you go through phases and explore the many different parts of your nature, you need the freedom to be able to move on and adapt. This can mean a steady succession of jobs, girlfriends and places to live, and you're too busy enjoying yourself to notice what you are leaving behind. Gemini men will find fulfilment through living life on your own terms, in a way others respect.

The Gemini woman is usually tall, slender with bright, penetrating eyes. You move quickly, with small, neat steps. When talking to others you are animated, and use your hands to make gestures. Like the men, you are youthful, and your face expresses a childlike curiosity.

you are more prepared to take on commitments than a Gemini man. You are romantic, but many relationships may come and go before you find someone who meets your requirements for a lasting bond.

The Geminian love of variety will express itself in your choice of clothes. You portray different images according to your mood, and others are amazed by the contrasting styles that you wear. Sometimes it takes friends a little while to realize who it is! Textures, colours and accessories are regularly combined with

ABOVE *You need plenty of stimulation, and study provides the perfect chance to stretch your mind and make new friends in the process.*

The Gemini woman is multi-faceted, and you need to express as many sides of your personality as possible. You have a very good mind, and love to use it. A career is important from an early age and you will probably change direction every so often. But you enjoy working and benefit from the feeling of security that it gives. Geminis like to study, and you often take courses in order to learn new skills.

You are independent, and love being out on the town, generally having a very active social life. Keeping up with the latest fashions, you resist getting old before your time, making a determined effort to stay young. This can make it hard for you to settle down, although

PRESENTS

- Gadgets of all kinds
- Tickets for movies or the theatre
- Books and magazines
- Computer software
- Word games, puzzles
- Fashion accessories
- Short trips
- Clocks
- Hand creams
- Novelty gifts

great success. However, Geminians do have to fight a tendency to mix too many styles at once, resulting in real clashes.

You love to shop for up-to-date clothes; magazines are a great source of ideas, to which you add your own inventive twists. Geminians know all the best places to shop, and some of the items you buy cost a fortune, while others are dirt-cheap. When it comes to accessories, you are a bit of a collector and love to scour flea markets for interesting and useful bargains.

Gemini women look especially good in classic clothes that show off their lithe and youthful figures. You probably have many pairs of shoes, some of them hardly worn. Varied accessories are also popular as you need to feel choices are available when preparing to go out.

Male Geminians steer clear of clothes that make them look too staid and conventional. You have a boyish charm, and select items that help you maintain your youthful image.

Both sexes can refuse to grow old gracefully, wearing outfits that are designed for someone much younger. But most Geminis avoid this, as your adaptable nature helps you look great whatever your age.

HEALTH

Geminians have a lot of vitality and energy. Your metabolism is fast and you burn many calories. Provided you pay attention to the demands of your body, you will enjoy above average health.

Geminians possess delicate nervous systems, and sometimes you lead life at such a hectic pace that there is a danger that you will become very tense and stressed out. It is important that you remember to slow down and take time to relax, and also make the effort to have regular meals. You will probably require more sleep than others, as your sensitive nerves need time to regenerate thoroughly.

The lungs are a potential weak point, and a cold can result in a nasty lingering cough. Wrap up against the elements, and perhaps take vitamins when winter arrives. The other areas of the body related to Gemini are the shoulders, arms and hands. These are vulnerable to injury, and sprains or broken bones may occur at some stage in your life. When you do suffer from ill health, you are a reluctant patient and will try to make light of your misfortune. Geminians recover fairly quickly, and it takes a serious illness to stop you from being restless.

Even if you don't spend much time at home, you like to be able to keep up your restless and varied lifestyle when you are there. Communication is vitally important, and you use your phone a lot. Computers are popular and you will have a good selection of books, newspapers and magazines. The TV is often on, if only in the background. Most Geminians like gadgets and technology and your living environment may be full of the latest utility and leisure appliances.

The general atmosphere of the Geminian home is bright and lively, with stimulating colour schemes and a clever use of space and light. Rooms often have more than one function, which reflects your ability to adapt. You have versatile furniture that can be easily moved, and you rearrange rooms whenever you feel like a change.

For most Geminians, location is more of a concern than the type of property. You like to be near the action; the hustle and bustle of a large metropolis is very attractive. Many Geminis get bored living in the country, and sooner or later move into a city. If you can, you find accommodation in the hippest part of town. Here you have access to an interesting variety of places to eat, shop and, of course, plenty of night life.

Geminians can find it hard to hold onto their cash. You make money easily, and often have more than one source

BELOW *A mid-fifteenth century French illustration of Gemini. Falconry was a summer sport and its depiction here simply indicates the time of year, not some Geminian qualities.*

of income; however, you also love spending it! Geminis are never at a loss for things to do and buy, as your interests are constantly evolving.

The boring, practical details involved with finance are difficult for you to take seriously. This can be a problem, as sometimes you neglect to pay bills, and may fail to keep your affairs in order. You have the funds, but you don't always use them well, since you are too busy getting on with the rest of your life!

A Geminian standard of living can fluctuate rapidly, as you may not know what you will be doing from one year to the next. Sometimes you use credit cards and loans to supplement your earnings, and can run up quite large debts without realizing it. Being organized is the key to financial success for the typical Geminian.

Investments work well if they are fun and can keep you interested. You are usually quick to spot opportunities and can make remarkably shrewd judgments, especially when you use your inquiring mind to read up on the subject.

Geminians love communicating, and you often spend time talking to others on the phone. Most of you possess a mobile phone, as you like to be in touch wherever you are. Reading and writing appeal, and you will sit for hours composing letters. Words fascinate you; Scrabble and crosswords are favourite pastimes. For many Geminians, spare

	How Gemini finds:		At a glance
♈ Aries		Lasting passion	❤❤❤❤
♉ Taurus		You must be kidding!	❤❤
♊ Gemini		Will it last?	❤❤❤❤
♋ Cancer		Possible...	❤❤❤
♌ Leo		True love	❤❤❤❤
♍ Virgo		Surprising success	❤❤❤❤
♎ Libra		Relaxing winner	❤❤❤❤❤
♏ Scorpio		Too intense	❤
♐ Sagittarius		Opposites attract	❤❤❤❤
♑ Capricorn		Most unlikely	❤
♒ Aquarius		Soul mates	❤❤❤❤❤
♓ Pisces		Too dreamy	❤❤

time is an opportunity to study, and you have a talent for picking up languages quickly.

Going out with friends gives you great pleasure, and you usually belong to a very active social circle. Bars, clubs, movies and galleries – you appreciate a wide variety of entertainment, and love sharing it with other stimulating minds.

You are interested in the media, and enjoy keeping up with the news; you are an ideal candidate for cable and satellite TV channels. You like technology and many Geminians derive tremendous enjoyment from their computer; especially the Internet. Global information 24 hours a day is a Gemini's idea of heaven!

You need variety, contrast and change, and feel restricted and frustrated if you don't get it. To break up your normal routine, you enjoy short breaks, perhaps staying with friends. You are not happy spending long periods of time by yourself, as

TRADITIONAL ASSOCIATIONS

Colours:
Yellow, black, white

Countries:
Armenia, Belgium, Sardinia

Tarot Card:
Number 6, the Lovers

Flowers:
Lily of the Valley

Birthstone:
Tourmaline, agate

Animals:
Magpie, small birds

Occupations:
Writers, TV presenters, Journalists

Herbs:
Caraway

Trees:
Nut-bearing trees

Cities:
Bruges, San Francisco, New York, Nuremberg

Food:
Nuts and seeds

Geminians thrive on companionship. Having nothing to do really gets you down, and you will go out of your way to keep busy and avoid boredom.

You start to feel trapped if you are forced to make too many commitments, as you prefer to keep your options open, always keeping one eye focused on the horizon.

RIGHT *Geminians love the diverse and fast-paced action of cities like New York.*

Cancer

Cancerians are known for having a tough, shell-like exterior that protects their very sensitive and vulnerable personalities from the world outside – just like the crab, in fact! Really, you're quite a softy, and because you have such delicate emotions, you need to feel safe. That is why you sometimes behave defensively.

You find it hard to be direct, preferring to approach things from an angle, advancing gradually. Once you have committed yourself emotionally to a course of action, however, you display great tenacity in reaching your goal, often surprising those around you in the process.

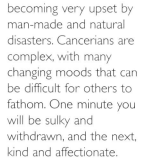

Family life is very important, and most Cancerians are extremely close to their next of kin – indeed, it is hard for you to feel secure unless relationships at home are good. Your childhood is always remembered, and it is here that you develop your instinctive need to care, which sooner or later will express itself in most areas of your life. You are so attached to the past that you sometimes fail to take advantage of current opportunities, and can have a tendency to dwell in nostalgia.

Cancerians are emotional and intuitive, with an almost psychic ability to pick up on how people are feeling and what is going on in their minds. You are also strongly attuned to nature, and care deeply about the environment, becoming very upset by man-made and natural disasters. Cancerians are complex, with many changing moods that can be difficult for others to fathom. One minute you will be sulky and withdrawn, and the next, kind and affectionate.

Once you learn to deal with your extreme sensitivity, it becomes an asset, and allows you to have a rich and emotionally fulfilling life.

The Cancerian man is inclined to be a little on the plump side; you have a round, moon-shaped face that conveys a variety of changing expressions. Dimples are common, and you have a ready smile. Your eyes are usually kind and sensitive, but you sometimes find it hard to meet the gaze of others.

You have a strong need for security, and will feel emotionally out of sorts if you don't have a comfortable place to live and money in your pocket.

Cancerians have a strong sense of privacy, and are usually very cautious when it comes to opening up to others, which is why a solid home base is fundamental to your well-being.

Many Cancerian men remain very attached to their mothers, and like to keep a close emotional bond for as long as possible. You are very creative and intuitive, and often make decisions based on your gut feelings. These usually turn out to be right, although you are sometimes guilty of waiting too long before acting on them!

ABOVE *Your affinity with water makes windsurfing a great sport to help you forget your troubles and lose yourself in the magic of the ocean.*

EXERCISE

You will benefit from regular exercise, as it helps you to relax and counters your anxiety. Cancerians are attracted to water sports, especially swimming. You like peaceful environments, and may prefer to arrive at the pool early, before the crowds arrive. Once you are comfortable with a set routine, you stick to it for many years.

Getting close to nature is popular, and many of you enjoy hiking and camping, often in wildernesses. Cancerians need periods of solitude, as these help recharge your batteries.

Having a family is something you will want to do at some stage. Cancerian men are very domesticated, and most women find this attractive. Ideally suited to the roles of husband and father, your business acumen ensures that everyone is well taken care of

Like Cancerian men, you have eyes that reveal a lot of emotion, and an expressive, often moon-shaped face. Your bone structure is generally strong, and according to your mood, you either slouch or carry yourself with an upright posture. Your body weight fluctuates, and you are often amply proportioned.

ABOVE *A cozy domestic scene that would warm many a Cancerian's heart. You enjoy having a close family with strong protective bonds.*

Cancerian women are ruled by their emotions, and you obtain much security through having close contact with friends and family. You can find it very frustrating if you are unable to express your caring nature, and get depressed if this goes on for a long time. You are very touchy and sensitive, and are quick to take offense, even though none may have been intended.

Creative and highly imaginative, you have a real talent for all forms of design. Cancerians are influenced by their subconscious, and your deep intuition gives you much insight into human nature. You have a strong sense of self-preservation, and use this for guidance when making decisions.

Cancerians are very maternal, and possess a very strong nesting instinct. Although you will probably have a successful career, you appreciate an intimate relationship more than most, and love having children and running a family home.

PRESENTS

- Beautiful shells
- Antiques
- Framed photos
- Food
- Something for the home
- Holidays near water
- Cookbooks
- Silver
- Binoculars
- Money

Cancerians can have problems in discovering what sort of look suits them best, as you choose clothes according to your mood. When it comes to actually buying new outfits, you can be reluctant to spend too much money, and will wait for as long as possible before renewing items in your wardrobe. Cancerians are shrewd, and quite content to wear hand-me-downs, often maximizing the overall effect with the addition of one or two carefully chosen accessories.

Although you have a great sense of colour and texture, you avoid dressing in a manner that attracts attention, preferring to create a subtle and slightly understated image. With your interest in the past, current fashion may leave you cold, and most Cancerians opt for traditional and conventional styles. Males can be surprisingly fussy about their appearance, and may take some time to get ready before going out. You favour well-cut suits and comfortable, stylish casuals. Sporty items are rarely worn, and you often look good in clothes with a nautical theme.

For work, women like dress suits, which help you feel comfortable and efficient. When relaxing, you prefer feminine clothes with gentle, flowing

HEALTH

Cancerians are very emotional, and your immune system is strongly affected by how you are feeling. When you are happy, your health will be exceptionally good. However, a bout of depression can leave you susceptible to everything that is going around. Essentially, you possess a tough and resilient constitution, and will recover from even serious illness with ease. Cancerians usually suffer in silence and rarely protest, despite the fact that you may be in great pain. You respond well to care and affection, as your body and mind are linked so strongly – feeling loved does more than anything else to assist a speedy return to health.

The main part of the body that relates to Cancer is the stomach. When you are upset, your digestion can be impaired, and it may be advisable to wait until you are calm before sitting down to eat. However, in general, you need to eat regular meals, as being hungry will put you in a bad mood, and can make it difficult for you to keep your poise.

For most Cancerians, happiness will do more than anything else to ensure good levels of health throughout your life.

ABOVE *This mid-fifteenth century illustration of Cancer the Crab is rather more like a lobster. The reaper again represents the activity of the season, not of the sign.*

lines. Dressing up is romantic, and you love to go out into the magic of night.

To a Cancerian, a home is a haven from the hustle and bustle of the world, a place where you can relax and really be yourself. You will go out of your way to create a cosy and familiar atmosphere there, and are happy to spend money to achieve this. The outside environment should also be peaceful and many Cancerians live in the country, as modern cities may be too stressful for your sensitive nature. You are drawn to properties that have some kind of history, and also like living near water.

Cancerians love collecting, and you will usually own some lovely pieces of antique furniture acquired over the years. Your passion for antiques often

results in large hoards of china and other collectibles, which can be positioned rather haphazardly from room-to-room. Cancerians are not known for their tidiness, and sometimes the overall effect is one of clutter. You love food and cooking, and the kitchen is likely to be large and well equipped. Gardening is another interest, and many of you will indulge your green fingers. Cancerians are very private and quick to defend your territorial rights, having little patience with nosy, obtrusive neighbours.

Cancerians are extremely cautious when it comes to money. This reflects your deep need to hold on to what you have, making you very careful and shrewd. On occasion, you will even hesitate before buying the simple necessities of life, as not having enough funds leaves you feeling exposed and vulnerable. You like money for the security it offers, and often devote a lot of time and energy to building up a large and substantial bank balance.

Cancerians are financially intuitive, and usually possess remarkable business acumen. Unless you have great respect for an expert, you would much rather keep control of your own financial affairs. Investments of all sorts appeal, but you will generally steer well clear of anything that appears risky and unpredictable. Many of you supplement your regular income with a hobby, such as buying and selling

antiques, or some other form of trade. Your judgement is superb, and many profitable careers spring from such ventures. As you get wealthier, you relax, and are more able to enjoy the good things in life, sharing these with family and close friends.

Because Cancerians love antiques and collecting so much, you may spend at least some of your free time rummaging around flea markets and car boot or garage sales, hoping to find something interesting to buy. If your hobby is more serious, your face will be a familiar sight at local auctions.

Cooking is usually one of your favourite pastimes, and you love to invite close friends over for a meal. Cancerians

		How Cancer finds:		At a glance
♈	Aries	Steamy affair		♥♥
♉	Taurus	Earthy winner		♥♥♥♥
♊	Gemini	Overly logical		♥
♋	Cancer	Deep love		♥♥♥♥♥
♌	Leo	Possible..		♥♥♥
♍	Virgo	Versatile bond		♥♥♥♥
♎	Libra	Different love concepts		♥♥
♏	Scorpio	Caring soulmates		♥♥♥♥♥
♐	Sagittarius	No way!		♥♥
♑	Capricorn	Lasting lovers		♥♥♥♥♥
♒	Aquarius	Too detached		♥
♓	Pisces	Non-stop romance		♥♥♥♥♥

use a lot of creative energy when preparing food, and like to add your own ideas to enhance established recipes. When you are feeling tense, cooking has a very relaxing effect, and does much to help you unwind. Cancerians also enjoy sailing and boating, as you have a natural affinity with water, and many of you like to go off on a fishing trip.

Being such a homebody, you are surprisingly fond of travel, and many of you have mobile homes so you can take all your creature comforts with you! Cancerians are very close to their relatives, and love to share free time and leisure activities with family members of all ages, especially when it comes to holidaying abroad.

You are very protective and defensive of your family, and react strongly to anyone who criticizes them. Cancerians have wonderful memories, and you appreciate birthday cards and people who remember special dates and anniversaries. Cancerians tend to be shy; loud and extrovert displays from others can make you feel self-conscious. If you live in a noisy location, this can also grate on your nerves, as more than anything else you need a tranquil home base.

TRADITIONAL ASSOCIATIONS

Colours:
Silver, indigo

Countries:
Canada,
The Netherlands,
United States

Tarot Card:
Number 7, the Chariot

Flowers:
Lotus

Birthstone:
Moonstone, pearl

Animals:
Crabs, frogs

Occupations:
Nurses, Antique dealers, Chefs, Interior designers

Herbs:
Lemon balm

Trees:
Alder, willow

Cities:
Istanbul, Venice
Amsterdam

Food:
Shellfish, lettuce, mushrooms

LEFT *Every once in a while your spirit benefits from a short period of total privacy, peace and seclusion.*

Leo

Leos are majestic and proud, and have a larger-than-life personality that needs to shine. You want to be in charge, and use passion and vitality to greet opportunities with enthusiasm. You are an extrovert with a tremendous love for life – a normal, humdrum existence is sure to disappoint whatever your age, you need plenty of drama and colour!

Leos have strong desires, and once you have set your mind on something, you display a burning determination to get your wish. This stubbornness can be your downfall, as Leos do not like changing course, and consequently, they occasionally persevere with a plan of action that is doomed to fail.

You have strong opinions on most subjects, and voice them with authority. Leos have a natural bravado, and you always sound as though you know what you are talking about, even if you don't! Others may find you dogmatic, but no one could accuse you of being weak-willed and indecisive.

As the lion of the zodiac, you like to feel that you are the king of the jungle and command respect. You can't stand it when people laugh at you, and your pride is easily hurt. In your own eyes you are a real celebrity, and you will go out of your way to achieve distinction and recognition in at least one area of your life. Leos have the potential to be real heroes, and are extremely brave and courageous, often achieving greatness in the face of enormous adversity.

Leos are self-possessed, and can often find it hard to let others have their say. You have a fiery strength that needs to be tempered, as sometimes you can simply overwhelm your friends and the people you meet. If you tone down your act on occasion, the world has much to gain from your warm and generous heart.

Most Leo men have short, broad backs with well-developed muscles. Your hair is often spectacular and curly, like a mane. You walk with a dignified posture, and dress to look good and attract admirers. Your voice is strong and commanding, and you are aware of your powerful sex appeal.

Leos are confident and charming, and you are used to getting your own way. You have grand visions and plans, and dislike those with petty, constricting attitudes. A born show-off, you can't

FOLIES-BERGÈRE

TOUS LES SOIRS

CHARMION

ABOVE *With its flamboyant costumes and feisty routines, the Folies-Bergère epitomises Leo's love of colour, drama and passionate energy.*

you decide to play the part of a loving husband. Your wife may need to allow you to be the focus of the marriage.

Leo women have slim, sensuous bodies, and are well-dressed whatever their personal circumstances. Even more than Leo men, your hair will be a real feature, probably with long, abundant curls that cascade down your back. You may have a superior expression, and will also dress to turn heads.

resist playing up to any audience that happens to be around, as you crave attention and need to feel loved and wanted. You have a taste for luxurious living, and like to indulge in the best, sometimes rather ostentatiously.

Leos want to be in control, and you will try and dominate your destiny whenever possible. You have fantastic will-power that gives you every chance of succeeding in this, although you have to watch a tendency to be too hard on yourself and others.

Honest and loyal, you take great pride in keeping your word. You love romance, and often have many admirers before

EXERCISE

Leos are very determined, and once you have committed yourself to an exercise programme you can stick to it religiously. Some Leos are lazy, but most usually enjoy expressing themselves through some form of physical activity.

Sports are popular, and you like to compete with yourself and others, always trying to improve your personal best. Team sports are often played, although you may insist on being captain. Leos love moving to music; aerobics and passionate Latin dances are very appealing. In caring for your back and posture, you may obtain good results with stretching exercises.

Leos have a lust for life and demand the best it has to offer. You will fight tooth and nail to get it, believing that luxury befits your regal nature. You need recognition and adulation from others, and want them to respond to your sunny disposition.

You are very passionate, and find it hard not to show emotion. Most of the time you will be fairly relaxed, but when you do lose your temper, the results can be quite frightening! You have a lot of self-respect, and do not take kindly to being pushed around. You are outgoing, and love to share

ABOVE *You enjoy showing off your good looks and flowing mane of hair.*

PRESENTS

- Gold jewellery
- Luxury clothes
- Fine champagne
- Dramatic films on video/dvd
- Art posters
- Designer clothes
- Holidays in hot climates
- Gourmet restaurants
- Tickets for a big show
- Beauty treatments

excitement and enjoyment with others, as your life force is too strong to keep to yourself. Relationships are very important, and you need a special man who is able to respect your dominant yet feminine personality. You feel most fully alive when you are in love.

Leos always dress to impress, no matter what the occasion! You love to look good, and feel enormous satisfaction when others glance in your direction. You are attracted to showy and often expensive clothes that help you stand out in a crowd. Anonymity is to be avoided at all costs, and if you really want to create a stir, you are quite prepared to splurge on something that may be worn only once or twice. Sometimes your desire to get noticed results in an image that is rather tacky, but you soon learn from your mistakes. Both sexes like to be glamourous, and designer labels appeal for both formal and casual wear.

Leo women like to dress for work in outfits that are smart, sexy and powerful. You are aware of the different roles in a career environment, and select a style that helps you achieve the desired impact. You are romantic, and love the drama of a big night out. As well as choosing your finest dress, you like classy perfume, and gold jewellery next to your skin. Leos usually bronze under the sun, and some keep their tans fresh with an occasional trip to the tanning bed. Leo men are also concerned with their appearance, and many spend hours on grooming. As you dislike looking unkempt, investing money on quality clothes is a real priority.

Leos are very proud, and you will do your best to make your home as splendid as possible. Even if it is quite a humble abode, you manage without fail to create an atmosphere that is warm, welcoming and a touch showy. You usually make sure that it is sparkling clean, and looking its best.

You like grand, palatial properties, and will get as big a place as your budget allows. Inside, you will probably

have sumptuous furniture and fittings, the more luxurious the better! Lush textures are favoured, and you love the feel of a deep, shag-pile carpet under your feet. Having a comfortable pad to relax in is important to you, and you love to entertain your guests in style.

BELOW *Conventionally in heraldry and other symbolic representations of the lion, the creature is shown, as here with an almost human face.*

Leos have a rich sense of colour, and you prefer bold interior designs, often featuring sunny shades of yellow and orange. A bright interior is a must, as you like your home to get as much light as possible, and may actually get depressed if it is too dark and gloomy. Good heating is another necessity as most Leos have a low tolerance for cold weather. Indeed, some of you are happy only when living in a hot climate.

Leos have a reputation for being extravagant, and you certainly enjoy living it up! Paying attention to detail is not your forte, and this sometimes results in your spending more than you earn. You can find it difficult to tighten your belt when required, and may borrow funds to enable you to carry on with your lavish lifestyle. Leos are attracted to the best, and do not cope well with poverty. Because of this, you are prepared to work very hard to attain a good level of material success, and many Leos become rich. Wealth helps you express your passion for life, and you can feel impotent without it.

HEALTH

You have a strong constitution that gives much protection against minor infections and complaints. Leos often take their health for granted, and you have to be careful of pushing yourself and working and playing so hard that you get run down. If illness does strike, you are genuinely surprised and almost affronted. You enjoy the attention of being a patient, but you also want others to know how strong you are, and make every effort to recover and get out of bed – sometimes far too quickly.

The heart and circulatory system is related to the sign of Leo, and when you become angry or stressed, your blood pressure can be high. Too many rich foods exacerbate this problem, and moderation in diet is thus advised. Men in particular are susceptible to heart disease if they persist with an over-indulgent lifestyle, so regular exercise is prudent, and will do much to ensure that later years are trouble-free.

The other main area of the body connected to Leo is the back, and you should try to walk as upright as possible. You are noble and proud, and find it hard to reveal your vulnerability. Because of this you can hold a lot of tension in your back muscles, so regular sit-ups or other exercises designed to strengthen lower-back muscles can be very beneficial.

When it comes to choosing investments, Leos are surprisingly conventional, preferring to put cash into something reliable and steady. You often seek expert advice to help you make the right decision. You have panache, and may invest in flamboyant enterprises, but this is usually when you have already built up substantial funds and even then it will be very carefully considered. Leos have a natural affinity with the stage, and you may like to get involved with backing a big show. Other areas that you could do well in include paintings and sculptures, and all forms of jewellery.

Leos have a tremendous zest for life, and love to go out and have a good time with friends. You love big events with lots of glitter and glamour, and will often unwind with a night on the town. With your sense of drama, the theatre and opera are natural choices, and you appreciate the chance to dress up and be seen – if some celebrities are present, so much the better, as you enjoy rubbing shoulders with the stars.

You have a taste for exclusive restaurants that serve gourmet foods and wines, dining whenever possible with close friends. Leos do not like eating out alone, as you need warm companionship. Shopping is another of your favourite pastimes, although you can feel very frustrated if you don't have the money to buy what you want.

	How Leo finds:		At a glance
♈	Aries	Hot stuff!	❤❤❤❤
♉	Taurus	Sometimes…	❤❤❤
♊	Gemini	Stimulating love	❤❤❤❤
♋	Cancer	Complementary	❤❤❤
♌	Leo	Non-stop passion	❤❤❤❤❤
♍	Virgo	Forget it	❤
♎	Libra	Romantic delight	❤❤❤❤
♏	Scorpio	All or nothing	❤❤❤
♐	Sagittarius	Yes!	❤❤❤❤❤
♑	Capricorn	Definitely possible	❤❤❤
♒	Aquarius	Do opposites attract?	❤❤❤
♓	Pisces	Steamy affair	❤❤❤

TRADITIONAL ASSOCIATIONS

Colours:
Sunny oranges, yellows

Countries:
France, Turkey, Italy, Bohemia

Tarot Card:
Number 11, Strength

Flowers:
Sunflowers

Birthstone:
Cat's eye, ruby

Animals:
Lions, domestic cats, lynx

Occupations:
Actors, Business executives, Models, Clothing designers

Herbs:
Marigold

Trees:
Orange, cedar, bay

Cities:
Rome, Prague Damascus

Food:
Rich meaty foods

RIGHT *Every Leo is a potential king and queen, and for a choice of somewhere to live, what could be more fitting than this fabulous and romantic palace!*

Leos often take up rewarding hobbies, and many of you are drawn towards joining an amateur dramatics group. Your creative talents also find fulfilment with painting, sculpture and jewellery-making, and you can surprise others with your professional results.

Given the choice, some Leos will do nothing more than laze around for hours like a cat! Pleasures of all sorts appeal, and receiving thoughtful and indulgent gifts from those you love makes you purr with real delight.

As you are a real sucker for flattery, an appreciative audience boosts your ego tremendously. Similarly, being ignored is sure to raise your hackles, and you hate being taken for a fool. If someone breaks your trust, your Leo pride may take some time to heal. You need to feel that your life is special, and can struggle if things become too mundane and drab.

Virgo

Practical and adaptable, Virgoans are discriminating, and have a strong desire to serve. You are critical of yourself and others, and often have impossibly high standards. Details matter to you, which is why you strive for perfection. A Virgoan's mind is a powerful tool, and you need to learn how to use it to your advantage.

You are helpful and sympathetic, always ready to lend a hand when required. Virgoans feel connected to humanity and spend much time working for the good of others, tending to put other people's needs before their own – even if it is inappropriate.

Your sharp insight and ability to probe allows you to see things that others miss, but also makes you inclined to worry, which can really hold you back. Self-doubt is your biggest enemy, but once this is conquered, there is no stopping you. Virgoans have many talents, and are surprisingly versatile.

Mentally, you can be quite delicate, and for you to feel secure, it is very important for the practical and material side of life to be in order. A good job is a necessity, as is financial stability Without these, it can be difficult for you to stop worrying.

Virgo is an often-misunderstood sign, as part of you is concerned with purity and cleanliness, and this can lead to a real obsession with health and hygiene. Indeed, some Virgoans are very prudish, and find all bodily functions distasteful. However, you are also very earthy and sensuous, with a fondness for the pleasures of the flesh and riotous good times with friends – a part of your more uninhibited, wild side that you may be afraid to express. For true happiness, you need to reconcile and integrate these two Virgoan extremes.

Virgoan men tend to be tall and straight; you walk with an upright posture, and place your feet on the ground with precise, considered steps. Your face has neat features, and you often give the impression of being deep in thought. Virgoans have a reputation for cleanliness, and you often look as though you have just washed and put on fresh clothes.

Virgoan men are pragmatic, and generally your head will rule your heart. You find it hard to relate to 'mushy' emotions, and as a result, prefer to stay cool and detached. You have a strong sense of responsibility, and are driven to seek fulfilment through your work.

Instinctively, you like to be busy, and your analytical mind needs plenty to keep it occupied. Without constructive outlets, you channel your energy into being negative and critical of the world at large. This is overcome by doing some sort of service, and for many Virgoans, personal happiness is linked to the welfare of others.

BELOW *These simple and deliciously healthy foods could well be found in your larder! You seem to thrive on a diet that is close to nature.*

EXERCISE

Virgoans like to be healthy, and you are usually motivated to exercise regularly. Being outside in the fresh air does wonders for your whole system, and walking, cycling and running are popular ways to keep fit. Indoors, you like dancing and aerobics, and with all sports, you work on perfecting technique. Virgoans can be very restless physically, and may suffer from nervous tension. Because of this, learning to be calm both in body and mind brings tangible and lasting rewards. Many Virgoans find meditation an effective way to relieve stress.

When it comes to getting involved romantically, you can be remarkably self-sufficient, and spend long periods of time on your own. However, falling in love does much to enrich your life.

Virgoan women usually have delicate bodies, and walk with small, dainty steps. Your hair is neat and well cut, and your dress tends to be immaculate, with fussy attention to detail. The features on your face are often sharp, and, when worried, the mouth and eyes can tense up. When relaxed, your whole expression melts, and you look noticeably younger.

Although you are shy and appear to be rather meek, this masks your inner qualities of determination and courage. You are often brutally honest, and are under no illusions about what you want

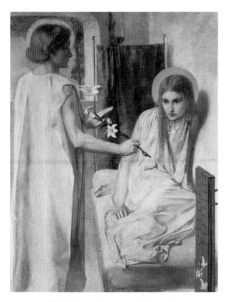

ABOVE *The Virgin Mary symbolizes honesty and purity – qualities associated with the sign of Virgo.*

quest for real love, often saving yourself until the right person comes along.

Some Virgoans are extremely unkempt, but most of you are immaculately groomed, and you take great care with your appearance. Whatever it is you are wearing, the overall effect is usually very neat and tidy. You avoid loose-fitting, baggy garments, choosing smart, functional outfits that will last. Virgoans are sensible, and you are prepared to shop around for a bargain, rather than risk the chance of overspending. When it

out of life and what will make you happy. You are prepared to sever many ties quite ruthlessly in your search for personal fulfilment.

You do have strong feelings, but it can be hard for you to show them, as you prefer to make decisions based on reason, and may find it difficult to trust your intuition. Virgoans have pure motives, but sometimes get so caught up with your sense of duty and need to serve that you sacrifice important ambitions, and later regret having let opportunities pass you by

You are surprisingly romantic, and can be quite uncompromising in your

PRESENTS
•••••••••••

- ● Organic foods
- ● Electronic organizer
- ● Books related to hobbies
- ● Tools
- ● Ornaments
- ● Alternative health products
- ● Trips to the country
- ● Fine stationery
- ● Arts and crafts items
- ● Cotton sheets

comes to matters of style, modesty and caution prevail, and you generally opt for fairly conventional trends.

Women favour blouses and skirts for work, often with greens, browns and greys. Accessories will be tidy and shoes are always freshly polished. You may take some time putting the finishing touches to your image, and then make readjustments as the day progresses. For leisure, you love relaxing in natural fibres, and have a weakness for a pretty dress. You also like to wear trousers, but never give a sloppy impression.

Men feel efficient and comfortable in a suit, and you can be quite meticulous about positioning your tie. White shirts are favoured, and are changed every day without fail. Clean clothes make you think more clearly, while dirty ones put you in a bad mood. For leisure, you prefer crisp sweat-suits and understated casuals. On rare occasions, you are quite experimental when dressing up.

Many Virgoans like to have modern homes, as these are much easier to run and clean. You prefer simple buildings, and do not like to live in anything too showy. You can find city life pretentious, and feel a lot more relaxed in a rural setting. However, modern careers mean this is not always possible, and you may have to settle for living within striking distance of the country.

HEALTH

Virgoans usually take an active interest in their bodies, and you are sensible enough to stay in tip-top condition. Your sometimes-delicate constitution benefits from such foresight, and provided you maintain a balanced approach and don't become too obsessive, you should enjoy good health for many years.

Worrying can make you prone to hypochondria, and small symptoms are often blown out of proportion.

A Virgoan's nervous system is very sensitive, and you find it hard to stay calm. When genuine illness strikes, you do everything within your power to fight it, persisting until recovery is absolute.

The main parts of the body connected to Virgo are the digestive tract and skin. When worried and uptight, you may become susceptible to irritable bowel syndrome and eczema-like complaints. Although eating the right foods can help, staying relaxed is much more effective.

ABOVE *Here Virgo is depicted as a young girl, in her left hand a palm branch, her right raised in blessing – or admonition.*

Virgoans have a taste for wood and other natural materials. Stripped floors and tiles are popular, and you have a preference for large rugs and drapes that can be easily moved around. You usually choose carpets that are highly practical and durable.

For decor, you like to create a bright atmosphere, and light colours are prevalent. Both sexes have home maintenance skills that you use to achieve a functional, cheerful design throughout your home, which is welcoming and relaxing for guests.

Some Virgoans have a tendency to be overly fussy, and you may fill your homes with lots of ornaments and knick-knacks, or grand displays of china that are cleaned regularly, but never used. You love to have a sense of order, but you can get carried away!

Virgoans are cautious and thrifty when it comes to spending cash. Even for minor purchases, you are liable to research them thoroughly to make sure that you get the best bargain. You don't see the point of shelling out money without good reason, and can be quite humble in your tastes.

Your attention to detail makes keeping track of finances simple, and you are unlikely to have debts. A few disorganized Virgoans do have chaotic, messy finances, but most of you are very careful, taking great comfort in knowing how even the smallest amount was spent. You provide for the future without really trying, as your modest lifestyle means that you usually live on much less than you earn.

Long-term security is important to a Virgoan, and you are generally very interested in investing. Slow, steady profits appeal, although sometimes you can be too cautious for your own good.

Virgoans are versatile, and keep busy with hobbies. These have every chance of developing into a viable business, although your desire for perfection can mean that you never believe your products are good enough to sell!

Virgoans really like to keep busy, and your leisure hours will usually find you engaged in some sort of fruitful activity. With your desire to help humanity, being involved in charity work is very fulfilling and a good way to make contact with like-minded others. You are generous with your time, and take your responsibilities seriously

Virgoans have sharp, lively brains, which you use to focus on one or two specialized interests. Whether academic or practical, these may develop into rewarding hobbies, and you can become a real expert in your field. You are skilled with crafts that require careful attention, such as needlepoint and model-making.

Gardening is popular, and it is also a very good way for you to unwind. Virgoans are keen students, and you are often found at evening classes, adding another string to your bow. You see your friends regularly, and really appreciate doing a variety of things with them.

	How Virgo finds:		At a glance
♈	Aries	Inconsiderate	❤❤
♉	Taurus	Lasting joy	❤❤❤❤❤
♊	Gemini	Surprise hit	❤❤❤❤
♋	Cancer	Caring partner	❤❤❤❤
♌	Leo	Absolutely not!	❤
♍	Virgo	Pragmatic soul mates	❤❤❤❤❤
♎	Libra	Too impractical	❤❤❤
♏	Scorpio	Good, but intense	❤❤❤❤
♐	Sagittarius	Restless mismatch	❤❤
♑	Capricorn	Everyone's a winner	❤❤❤❤❤
♒	Aquarius	Keep walking!	❤
♓	Pisces	Compassionate love	❤❤❤❤

RIGHT *Meditation can be very beneficial as it helps you to keep your inner poise and to soothe frayed nerves.*

TRADITIONAL ASSOCIATIONS

Colours:
Browns and greens

Countries:
Greece, Switzerland

Tarot Card:
Number 9, the Hermit

Flowers:
Buttercup

Birthstone:
Peridot, sardonyx

Animals:
Mice, insects

Occupations:
Accountant's, Scientist's, Teachers, Writers

Herbs:
Lavender

Trees:
Elder, nut-bearing trees

Cities:
Heidelberg Boston, Baghdad, Geneva

Food:
Wheat and rice

When they come to dinner, you are likely to prepare your latest health food recipe.

Virgoans don't like it when they feel as though life is becoming disorganized and unmanageable. You want to know precisely what needs to be done, and love making lists to clarify tasks. You can be very picky, and become quite upset if others fail to live up to your exacting standards of tidiness and cleanliness.

Being bored makes you fidgety, and you try always to keep busy. You find irresponsible and immodest behaviour really annoying, and have little time for those who make a habit of saying one thing and doing another. For a Virgoan, humility and consistency are very important.

Libra

The sign of Libra is ruled by the scales. You are thoughtful and sensitive, and seek balance and harmony whenever possible. Librans need people more than other signs, and sometimes find it difficult to be alone; good relationships with others are the key to your happiness and security

Intellectual and refined, you think very carefully before making decisions, preferring to weigh all the pros and cons of any situation. Sometimes you prefer to sit on the fence rather than commit yourself to one side. You enjoy discussions and arguments, and will often take the opposing view to make a conversation more interesting. This can infuriate others, who never know where you really stand!

 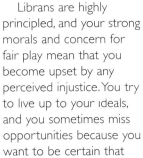

You are also diplomatic and charming, with a real gift for being able to listen and sympathize. This ability to communicate well makes you very sociable, and you usually have lots of friends. However, you can be a bit of a people pleaser, and may compromise yourself in the process.

Librans dislike creating waves and, as a result, you often store up problems rather than face any form of unpleasantness. But occasionally you can benefit from confronting issues head on. You present an image of poise and calm to the outside world, but this laid-back persona masks how much you are affected by what goes on around you.

Librans are highly principled, and your strong morals and concern for fair play mean that you become upset by any perceived injustice. You try to live up to your ideals, and you sometimes miss opportunities because you want to be certain that you have made the right decision. Once you have learned to trust and act on your instincts, you become a doer as well as a thinker.

The typical Libran man has a pleasing face, which maintains a serene expression even when upset or angry. Your bone structure is usually delicate, and your hair very fine. You walk with graceful and thoughtful steps, and are conscious of your appearance, grooming yourself carefully before going out.

Librans are blessed with abundant social skills, and your wit and charm ensure popularity. You love exploring ideas and concepts, and really enjoy lively conversations with others. You usually have plenty of advice to give, but aren't always so good at practicing what you preach!

Libran men have a strong feminine side, and therefore relate easily to the opposite sex from an early age. You are artistic, and appreciate many forms of beauty, in fact, your love for the finer things in life can make you quite indulgent in your pursuit of pleasure. You are prone to laziness, which should not be left unchecked.

ABOVE *Hiking with friends is the perfect way for you to keep fit. Sharing such outdoor activities makes them far more enjoyable to you.*

EXERCISE

You can be quite lazy when it comes to exercising regularly, and any fitness routine must be fun to sustain your interest. Librans dislike being uncomfortable, and are not suited to punishing fitness programmes. Walking, swimming, and dancing are all popular with Librans, and you find them far more enjoyable when done with friends. Many Librans take up t'ai chi, as you appreciate the concept of yin and yang, with its emphasis on the balance of body and mind. As you desire to look good, you may join a health club – you enjoy pampering yourself, and your vanity is a powerful spur to getting fit and staying in shape.

A strong partnership is vital for you to feel complete. You have a great need for intimacy, and a loving relationship brings you deep and lasting fulfillment.

Libran women have well-proportioned and generally attractive features. You tend to be slim, with a curvy figure and fairly broad hips. Like Libran men, your face displays serenity and poise even in times of crisis, and you move with elegance and grace. You are very aware of how you look, and like to check mirrors for reassurance.

You possess an excellent mind, and are more than capable of holding your own in sharp debates. You are at your best when working with others, as occasionally you require a second opinion to make a decision. Librans are very tactful, and people find it easy to trust you and relax in your company.

Your gentle, subtle manner disguises a fierce determination – the original 'steel magnolia'! When necessary, you can be really tough and forthright in achieving your aims. You crave creature comforts, and may find it hard to do without. Libran women usually require beauty and tranquillity before they can really relax and unwind. You are very romantic, and have a tremendous amount of love and energy to put into

ABOVE *You usually enjoy looking at your own reflection – sometimes too much for your own good!*

PRESENTS

- Flowers and chocolates
- Romantic meals
- Beauty products
- CDs and tapes
- Stereo and camera equipment
- Pampering at a health club
- Luxury gifts
- Surprise parties
- A relaxing cruise
- Quality clothes

a relationship. You do not enjoy being alone, and if single, you will actively seek a partner. Of all the signs of the zodiac, Librans truly find themselves through others.

Librans are very image-conscious, and are concerned about wearing the right clothes. You can take a lot of time preparing to go out, and you will often try on different outfits and then change your mind at the last minute! Some Librans become obsessed with preening and dressing themselves, and can be quite vain and narcissistic.

Most of you have good taste, and coordinate outfits harmoniously, usually avoiding clashes of style and colour. Romantic looks are favoured by both sexes, and you are happy to spend money to keep your wardrobe well stocked. Fashionable clothes usually look good on you, provided they are not too hard and aggressive, as you prefer soft textures and tones that subtly enhance your attractiveness and presence.

At work, women are at their best in slightly formal styles. If you choose something too casual, the overall effect may be inappropriate. When dressing up, Libran women look stunning wearing flowing dresses in pastel shades. You like to add a splash of individuality with accessories, and fragrant perfumes complement your romantic mood. Even in jeans and casuals, female Librans look very feminine.

Male Librans can be quite fashionable in their choice of work clothes, selecting suits with real pizzazz. Although for some casual wear you can be surprisingly unfussy, you will always dress up for an important date since romance is something you take very seriously indeed!

Librans hate noise and clutter, and your well-developed aesthetic sense means that you are adversely affected by harsh and unattractive environments. If possible, you prefer to live in a beautiful area, but you will do your utmost to make wherever you call home tranquil and harmonious.

HEALTH

Librans stay healthy provided they keep their body balanced. However, you can find it hard to resist indulgent living. Too many late nights and constant rich foods mean that you will become run down easily, and if you do not take remedial action, illness may result. Be kind to your system, and most minor ailments simply disappear.

The kidneys and liver are the main body areas related to the sign of Libra. Your sensitive body can become stressed quite easily. When this happens, these vital organs may not function at their normal efficiency, and you may experience a buildup of toxins, resulting in headaches and chronic tiredness. Most of these symptoms will be alleviated by taking it easy and eating light foods that don't place a strain on your digestive system. When your energy levels recover, light exercise is advisable.

As some Librans are prone to a sluggish metabolism, a moderate diet is very important. If you do become ill, beautiful surroundings and plenty of attention from friends is guaranteed to aid the healing process; being isolated can make you more susceptible to disease.

RIGHT *Libran Oscar Wilde was renowned for his elegant and sophisticated wit.*

You are skilled at creating an atmosphere that is gently relaxing, using soft furnishings and warm designs to create a feeling of peace and comfort. Librans like balance in their homes, and will try to arrange the furniture in every room to achieve a sense of proportion and space. You also experiment with lighting, using dimmer switches, candles and spotlights to set the desired mood.

Because clutter grates on your nerves, you will tidy up and do the household chores on a regular basis, although you may hire help if you can afford it. You use your natural good taste to beautify your home, and make it an enjoyable and special place for others to visit. Being able to offer hospitality is very important, as you won't be happy if you are always stuck at home alone. Living in a remote area is unlikely to appeal to you, as you need to feel that you are accessible to your friends.

Librans like to maintain a good standard of living, and may find it difficult to economize. This can result in overdrafts and large credit-card debts before you realise the seriousness of the situation and finally take decisive action to put things right. You are resourceful and earn money with ease, but you may experience problems as a result of your somewhat relaxed and carefree attitude towards money management – a little prudence and self-control will do much to ensure your continued prosperity

You enjoy spending money on luxuries, and are very generous to friends and family. You can be easily swayed by a hard-luck story, and should be wary of those who try to take advantage of your kindness.

Librans will cheerfully work with diligence to fund their preferred lifestyle, but learning the details of various investment plans may bore you to tears. If you find it difficult to make decisions about your future financial plans, seeking professional advice is strongly recommended.

Joint business ventures with friends can work out well, particularly if they are based on a genuine interest rather than just a whim. You enjoy shared responsibility, as your motivation is generally much stronger when others are involved.

Librans are very sociable and prefer to spend their leisure time with others, so rather than doing something on your own, you usually invite a friend along. Art exhibitions, movies, nightclubs and concerts are your favourite ways to socialize. You love discussing what you have seen and done by relaxing over dinner with friends.

Many Librans are very musical, and as well as attending performances, you may play an instrument yourself. Your CD or album collection is likely to be large, as listening to music is a favourite way for you to unwind. You prefer harmonious tunes that create a tranquil atmosphere.

Librans have a gentle creativity that can be hard to express in words. Photography and painting may attract you, as you are drawn towards capturing images of beauty Once you have found

	How Libra finds:		At a glance
♈	Aries	Perfect blend	❤❤❤❤❤
♉	Taurus	Every so often	❤❤❤
♊	Gemini	Smashing!	❤❤❤❤❤
♋	Cancer	Unlikely	❤❤
♌	Leo	Plenty of passion	❤❤❤❤
♍	Virgo	Overly practical	❤❤❤
♎	Libra	Balanced love	❤❤❤❤
♏	Scorpio	Too much!	❤
♐	Sagittarius	Yes!	❤❤❤❤❤
♑	Capricorn	Definitely not	❤
♒	Aquarius	Air sign delight	❤❤❤❤❤
♓	Pisces	Possibilities	❤❤❤

something that you really like, you study it seriously, and it may develop into a life-long hobby or career.

Librans are quite inclined to laziness, and periodically take a complete break from any form of activity This quickly recharges your batteries, and it won't be long before you start calling your friends!

You enjoy verbal banter, and are frustrated if someone always agrees with you. You can have quite a lot of stored aggression, and arguing provides a positive channel for its release. Librans need plenty of time to reach a decision, and being forced to make up your mind before you are ready makes you feel quite stressed. You love easy-going environments that allow you to really relax. Librans need attention, but generally avoid the spotlight. Lack of human contact can lead to depression and for happiness, nothing beats warm, solid friendships.

TRADITIONAL ASSOCIATIONS

Colours:
Pale blue, pink

Countries:
China, Austria

Tarot Card:
Number 8, Justice

Flowers:
Mallow

Birthstone:
Sapphire, emerald

Animals:
Swans

Occupations:
Counsellors, Creating music, Lawyers, Psychologists

Herbs:
Aloe

Trees:
White sycamore, fig

Cities:
Frankfurt, Vienna, Copenhagen, Arles

Food:
Milk, honey, fruit

RIGHT *Classical music gives you a chance to express your aesthetic sensibilities.*

Scorpio

The depth and intensity of your emotions gives you an inner power that demands expression. Scorpios are creatures of passion, and your focused desires help you to achieve your aims. Mysterious and fearless, you are willing to undergo total transformation when necessary, rising like the phoenix to claim new life.

Scorpios have a penetrating insight, always seeking what lies beneath the surface. You can be ruthlessly self-critical in your quest for truth, understanding only too well what makes you tick. Your perceptive mind enjoys investigating all aspects of human nature, including many that are taboo. The resulting awareness of your own motivations produces a healthy suspicion of other people, and sometimes you take this to extremes, becoming very reluctant to trust anyone.

You have an excellent memory for how things have affected you on an emotional level. Scorpios have an inherent sense of justice and loyalty and your fixed nature means that you hold onto hurts and betrayals for a long time. Deep-seated bitterness may make it hard to dispel vengeful thoughts, and you are patient and secretive when plotting revenge.

Scorpios are uncompromising, and when a commitment is made, you promise your all and stick to it. You need to feel good about what you are doing, and clear goals are very important, because you hate feeling as if you are in limbo. Emotional fulfilment is absolutely vital, and if you don't have it in one area, you will seek it in another.

Scorpios have a charismatic, magnetic presence that usually attracts the attention of others. Your deep sexuality provides the source of your tremendous energy. Whether you use this creative force for good or evil is a moral dilemma that only you can solve.

The typical Scorpio man has strong features with penetrating, hypnotic eyes. Your body hair is likely to be thick and abundant, and your heavy eyebrows often meet in the middle. You walk with confident, purposeful steps, and usually have a broad, well-muscled chest. Your sex appeal is usually obvious, and many women find it hard not to steal a glance as you pass by.

You have strong opinions, and plunge yourself into life with abandon. Scorpios are fearlessly honest, and this can sometimes compel you to confront others with the truth. You are master of your own destiny and react violently to unwelcome interference You like to explore the full range of human desire, including the darker sides!

Scorpios have the potential to transform their nature, and you will probably go through two or three complete life changes, each time emerging wiser and more whole. These periods can be very testing, but they

ABOVE *Highboard diving provides intense excitement – a vital ingredient if exercise is to hold your interest.*

EXERCISE

Insufficient exercise can leave you feeling emotionally out of balance. Scorpio's intense nature needs demanding physical challenges, and the martial arts and other tough sports give a positive outlet for potentially dangerous levels of aggression. Aerobics, jogging and working out in a gym help to release tension and tone your body. You are also attracted to water sports, especially swimming and scuba diving. Scorpios love going down into the depths of the sea to discover another dimension of experience.

are a necessary part of your evolution. The reward for undergoing such trials is a real sense of peace and freedom, something you instinctively seek. You love sharing your intense emotions in a relationship, and need a woman who can handle your powerful blend of passion and control.

The typical Scorpio woman is sultry, and well aware of her sex appeal. You have magnetic eyes that command attention, with a body that is curvy and strong. You have a tangible physical presence. Scorpios usually have a sixth sense and an ability to read people's minds, which some may find unnerving.

Scorpio women exude confidence and control. Inside you may be a torrent of emotion, but you are careful not to let down your guard. Thoughtful

ABOVE *Many Scorpios have a nose for fine wines, and you particularly enjoy a rich, full-bodied red!*

man, however, you have the courage to let go and express your deepest self.

Scorpios like to wear clothes that emphasize your natural magnetism, and you can be quite bold with your image. You are comfortable with your sexuality, and not afraid to show it. Dark colours are favoured, and these give you an air of mystery and allure. In your quest to look good, you are prepared to spend money on quality items, but would rather go without than buy something that you are not completely taken by. You follow your own rules where trends are concerned, but are unlikely to stray too far from conventional styles.

and intuitive, you are interested in the deeper issues of life, having little time for shallow beliefs and superficial behaviour. You take full responsibility for your actions, and answer to no one.

You have many passions and talents, and it can be difficult to decide which to focus on. Once your goals are set, you persevere with remarkable spirit and conviction until success is achieved.

Scorpio women are tough and resilient, yet also extremely feminine. This combination sets you apart, and makes you very choosy when it comes to relationships. You are naturally dominant and assertive, liking to stay in control of your feelings. With the right

PRESENTS

- Sexy underwear
- Exotic food and drink
- Perfumes
- Erotic prints
- Massage oils
- Films and books with mystery
- Camera
- Metal detector
- Precious stones
- Trip to a nightclub

HEALTH

Scorpios have plenty of stamina and a highly resilient constitution, which means that your general health is usually good. You tend to take this for granted, and can push yourself to the absolute limit with excessive work and play. Your vital force is strong, but needs to be respected.

Some of the illness you experience is psychosomatic in origin, relating to blocked energy in your life. If this happens, you should try and recognize what is happening, and then act accordingly. Scorpios are prone to nervous tension, and this can affect muscles in the shoulders, neck and back. These respond well to massage and total relaxation.

The main parts of the body related to the sign of Scorpio are the reproductive organs, bladder and large intestine. It's important for you to eliminate toxins regularly – short, cleansing diets are very conducive to maintaining optimum health levels.

Scorpio women enjoy looking glamourous and sexy. If it is important to project a powerful image at work, you will dress effectively, and are not averse to using your looks to your advantage. When you want to relax, your choice of clothes depends on your mood – one day you may wear loose-fitting casuals, and the next, skin-tight leather trousers with a revealing top. For a really hot date you dress imaginatively, with confidence, daring, and flamboyance, using make-up and perfume to add a splash of magic.

For work, men prefer well-cut suits, and if you can afford it, these will be the best designer labels. In your leisure hours, you enjoy wearing manly casuals; When you really want to impress the opposite sex, you choose stylish clothes that maximize your charisma.

Privacy is important to a Scorpio, and you need to have a home where you can unwind and not be disturbed. You are fond of old buildings with character, and are quite sensitive to atmosphere. A prospective house or apartment has to have the right 'feel' before you will contemplate moving in.

Some Scorpios prefer to live in the country, and you are also very attracted to water. Your stormy nature finds solace near rivers and lakes. However, as most of you like to have plenty going on around you, only a city will do for the majority.

Scorpios have very distinctive ideas about decorating and furnishing their homes. Strong, vibrant colour schemes with predominant dark tones are popular. You love plush sofas and chairs, with rich fabrics such as silk, velvet, and satin for curtains and drapes. The overall effect is often quite exotic and intense, and you enjoy spending time creating something special.

Scorpios don't like too much bare space, and instead of having vast expanses of blank walls, you prefer to hang tasteful pictures and photographs. When entertaining, you use lights and mirrors to help vary the mood, and to create a feeling of intimacy for your guests.

Scorpios have a need for self-preservation, and are very careful with finances. Even when circumstances are difficult, you always seem to get by. Your intuition finds plenty of ways to make money, and you possess a strong desire to be rich. Sometimes you are very jealous of others, and forget to count your blessings; but usually you will work extremely hard in order to achieve success.

Scorpios really enjoy spending, and love the power that wealth provides. Once you are secure and settled, you can be extremely generous. Although you like to keep tight control of your funds, you have a good nose for

BELOW *Scorpio, as depicted in a series of zodiacal signs in the interior of an Egyptian mummy case of the second century A.D.*

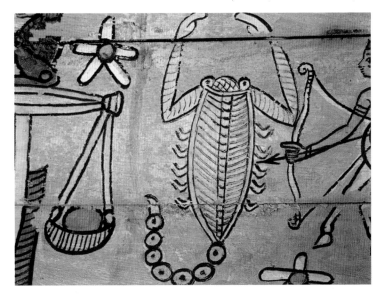

successful investing. Before making any decisions, you investigate various options in depth, and then make commitments. You are prepared to take considerable risks, and on occasion display a killer instinct.

Many of you consider running a business or being self-employed. A born survivor, you are able to transform and adapt when others would go under. Scorpios are competitive, and you thrive in the dog-eat-dog environment of modern trade. Answering only to yourself is very appealing, and psychologically, you have much to gain from being in charge of your own livelihood.

Leisure time is very precious to you, and it isn't wasted! Many Scorpios actively pursue pleasure, and your social life is usually rich and varied. Bars, nightclubs and lively parties make you feel really alive. You get a buzz from intense, exciting environments.

Scorpios enjoy having a few close friends who have different interests, and getting together with them is your favourite way to unwind after a stressful day. You appreciate good food and drink, especially when shared with others, and you may become absorbed in studying wine as a hobby. You have a reflective and imaginative side which is drawn to reading and watching movies.

	How Scorpio finds:		At a glance
♈	Aries	Passionate fling	❤❤❤
♉	Taurus	Winning attraction	❤❤❤❤
♊	Gemini	Forget it!!	❤
♋	Cancer	Water sign perfection	❤❤❤❤❤
♌	Leo	Very good or very bad	❤❤❤
♍	Virgo	Easygoing love	❤❤❤❤
♎	Libra	Uncommitted	❤
♏	Scorpio	Right on!	❤❤❤❤
♐	Sagittarius	Fun affair	❤❤❤
♑	Capricorn	Rock-solid romance	❤❤❤❤❤
♒	Aquarius	Sometimes lasts	❤❤❤
♓	Pisces	Deep	❤❤❤❤❤

TRADITIONAL ASSOCIATIONS

Colours:
Dark red, black

Countries:
Tibet, Morocco, Norway

Tarot Card:
Number 13, Death

Flowers:
Amaryllis

Birthstone:
Opal, turquoise

Animals:
Scorpions, eagles, lizards

Occupations:
Doctors, Bankers, Pharmacists, Financial analysts

Herbs:
Witch hazel

Trees:
Blackthorn, birch

Cities:
Cincinnati, Fez, Washington, D.C.

Food:
Meat and spicy foods

RIGHT *Scorpios are fascinated by the mysteries of the occult and by the unknown.*

Scorpios love anything to do with crime detection, mystery and the occult, so books and movies on these topics are fascinating to you. Occasionally, you need to be still and silent, as serious moods give you an urge to be on your own. Periods of inner communion are very necessary for your well-being.

Scorpios like to keep their thoughts private, and you are very uncomfortable in situations that force you to reveal personal, intimate information. But you have no qualms about probing the hidden secrets of others, and relish the chance to ask leading questions.

Your emotions are powerful, and you enjoy feeling that they are under control. Scorpios get depressed without action, and need to live at a pace that is emotionally charged.

Sagittarius

Sagittarians are both restless and visionary, and love to explore new horizons. You have a bold and optimistic attitude, and treat life as a journey full of adventure. Your enthusiasm and positive outlook often attract good fortune. Whatever you encounter along the way is greeted with a warm heart, an open mind and a ready smile.

Sagittarians have an expansive nature that needs to reach out and discover new challenges. This can be on a mental level, as an eternal student always thirsty for fresh knowledge, or on a physical level, with a strong passion for travelling the world. Most Sagittarians try to combine both elements.

Sagittarians are honest and frank, and have a reputation for giving an opinion even if it's not required. Occasionally, you are known to put your foot in your mouth with an untimely, tactless remark. Essentially well-meaning, you generally get away with these social blunders, and others rarely hold a grudge. You make decisions based on impulse and intuition, tempered by the wisdom of your own personal philosophy. Sagittarians are inclined to take risks, and you love stretching yourself by jumping into the unknown – although sometimes you fall flat on your face! However, you usually land on your feet, and quickly bounce back from any mistakes.

Most Sagittarians are idealistic, with a keen interest in the culture and beliefs of other countries. You ask probing questions about morality and social issues, sometimes developing passionate convictions. When this happens, you must watch a tendency to preach blindly to everyone in sight.

Sagittarians like movement, and if you feel that your life is stagnating you soon become bored and start looking around for a way to escape. Your spirit longs to be free.

Sagittarian men usually have tall, athletic bodies, and no matter what your height, your thighs are sturdy. You walk with wide strides, frequently swinging your arms. Your eyes are full of vitality and usually have a slight hint of mischief. You have a humourous expression, and your whole face lights up whenever you laugh.

You are at heart a bit of a gambler, and occasionally can be quite reckless. This wild side sometimes causes you to throw caution to the wind in order to test your inner strengths. You enjoy being physical, and are attracted to the great outdoors. Confined spaces can quickly bring on feelings of claustrophobia, and will suffocate your basic lively nature.

Your restlessness and desire to seek new challenges means it may be some time, if ever, before you are really ready to settle down. Sagittarians have to struggle to keep commitments, otherwise there is a danger of having too superficial a lifestyle.

You possess a great sense of humour, and are always glad to share a joke with others. Bold and confident,

ABOVE *This snowboarder is displaying the Sagittarian love of speed, adventure and risk.*

EXERCISE

Sagittarians enjoy team sports, and regular exercise. Football, baseball, hockey, wrestling, volleyball and basketball are favourites, whereas quieter pursuits such as golf or bowling may be a little too tame. You need to feel you've had a good work-out, and like the sensation of physical competition.

Sagittarians love hiking and camping in the mountains, taking in the scenery and breathing the fresh air. If you are seeking something more exciting, try skiing, snow boarding or surfing.

your extrovert approach is inspiring too. For you, fulfilment is reached through acting on your instincts. Sagittarian men are romantic, and love the companionship of women.

The Sagittarian woman has a striking face, often with handsome features. Your body is lithe, and, like the men, your thighs are well developed. Your eyes are bright, and your expression is frank and honest. You have a hearty appearance and walk with confident, uninhibited steps, looking directly ahead.

Strong and independent, Sagittarian women are the gypsies of the zodiac. You feel compelled to follow your passions, and can roam far and wide in

ABOVE *Unusual and exotic cultures appeal to your desire for mental as well as physical exploration.*

woman, and need a self-assured partner who makes you feel both loved and free.

Sagittarians are attracted to casual, unrestrictive clothes. It can be quite an ordeal stuffing yourself into formal attire, and you avoid this whenever possible. You faithfully stick to trusted items, often grabbing the first thing that comes to hand. The result is a slightly carefree image, for you rarely spend time on careful grooming.

Many Sagittarians put off buying new clothes until absolutely necessary – when you finally do so, your purchases are usually hasty and impulsive, with your search for happiness. Wherever you decide to call home, freedom of expression is always important, and you rebel against the constraints of convention. Sagittarians think for themselves, and you are always ruled by your own moral code.

You are very honest, and wear your heart on your sleeve. This openness gives you a certain vulnerability but it is also your greatest asset. After a few hard knocks, you learn to take care and avoid real trouble.

Relationships are one area where you must be careful, as your extreme optimism and impulsiveness can result in disappointment. You are a powerful

PRESENTS

- Plane or train tickets
- Books on travel
- Weekend in a country inn
- Case of vintage wine
- Evening college classes
- Car accessories
- Adventure sports
- Internet modem
- Comedy shows
- A day at the races

only a cursory search for a bargain. These shopping expeditions often result in mistakes and some garments may have to be exchanged.

Female Sagittarians are attracted to country styles that reflect their preference for an outdoor life. If forced to dress up for work, you prefer to wear interesting colours. For relaxing, you enjoy the comfort of sweatsuits, and these often become like a second skin. A romantic evening gives you a chance to show your bohemian soul, and you respond by dressing exotically.

Sagittarian men will often wear a loud, colourful tie when confined in a suit. This twist of humour is typical. Leisure wear is usually sporty, and you favour generously cut casuals that have a free, easy feel. For a really big date, you are prepared to change your style and submit to formal clothes.

Sagittarians have a strong affinity for the country, and many of you make your homes there. You love wide open spaces and the freedom of the wilderness. City life with all its pollution, noise and intense population can be

HEALTH

Sagittarians have active, physical lifestyles that keep them robust and healthy. You like to move around and use your body, and this precludes most minor ills from affecting you. On the rare occasions when you do fall ill, you concentrate intensely on getting well, as you find being a patient incredibly dull. Such a tendency usually means a quick recovery, and you display a cheerful optimism even when in pain.

The parts of the body connected to your sign include the liver, hips and thighs. A weakness for rich foods and wines may lead to plumpness,

especially in middle age. To get rid of these fatty areas, vigorous activity must be combined with a sensible diet. You have a very indulgent streak that can tax your liver's ability to cope.

In later years, arthritis and rheumatism can affect your hips. Modest exercise offers some protection, as does avoiding prolonged exposure to damp. Sagittarians can be a trifle clumsy, resulting in various bumps and bruises.

Experience will teach you to be extra careful when rushing around. Your love for reckless sports also provides potential for serious accidents. Although lucky, you would be wise not to push your luck too far.

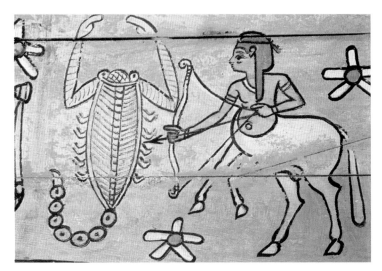

stifling, and you are often forced to go for a drive to keep your sanity.

Any apartment or house, no matter what its location, must have a feeling of space, light and air, with plenty of room to breathe. You find small, stuffy apartments depressing, and will gladly spend extra money to secure the right place. Sagittarians like simple, no-non-sense furniture and basic curtains and rugs. You are not inclined towards fancy interior designs, and prefer one or two very simple colours as decoration.

Sagittarians, not known for their tidiness, prefer to relax at home without worrying about making a mess. Artifacts from different cultures may be scattered about, revealing your love for travel. You are very sociable, and an affable host. Your spare bed is likely to be well used, as friends are always invited to stay.

ABOVE *Scorpio and Sagittarius painted on the inside of an Egyptian mummy case of the second century A.D. The tradition of depicting the Archer as a centaur, half man, half beast, seems as old as the sign itself.*

Sagittarians are by nature extravagant, and you may find that despite your best intentions, money slips through your fingers. You have little desire to scrutinize your finances, and your impulsive approach can mean that sometimes debts are incurred at a rather alarming rate. But hope springs eternal, and you always believe that more funds will arrive, even if there is nothing on the horizon. However, you generally work hard, though, and put in enough overtime to balance the books.

Sagittarians are very generous, and happily share their wealth – occasionally with people who take advantage. You hate being miserly, and feel sorry for those who are. Inside every Sagittarian is a potential gambler. This may never surface, but if it does, you could develop a serious addiction to racing, casinos or others forms of betting.

When it comes to investing, you find wild speculation very attractive, and more than one Sagittarian has gotten burned this way. In the right environment, your gambling instincts are very assured, especially in conjunction with expert tips. You need a slight sense of risk and adventure, finding things such as safe pensions and saving plans rather boring. Sagittarians are generally lucky, and have a way of stumbling into money.

Sagittarians like to make full use of all available leisure time. You have plenty of energy for work and play, preferring to have at least a few evening activities planned each week. Natural students, you jump at the chance to branch out into new fields of knowledge, and can be very disciplined when you discover a subject that really fires your imagination. Favoured topics are languages, religions, anthropology, sociology and philosophy.

A gregarious party animal, you also certainly know how to relax and have fun! Your friendliness puts others at ease, and most Sagittarians have a large circle of friends. You can be quite bawdy after a couple of drinks, and keep everyone amused with your jokes and tall stories!

		How Sagittarius finds:	At a glance
♈	Aries	Love perfection	❤❤❤❤❤
♉	Taurus	Hidden flaws	❤
♊	Gemini	Strong attraction	❤❤❤❤
♋	Cancer	Once in a blue moon	❤❤
♌	Leo	Feel the heat!	❤❤❤❤❤
♍	Virgo	Real clash	❤❤
♎	Libra	Sweet and lasting	❤❤❤❤❤
♏	Scorpio	Short-term sizzler!	❤❤❤
♐	Sagittarius	Gypsy passion	❤❤❤❤❤
♑	Capricorn	No!	❤
♒	Aquarius	Yes!	❤❤❤❤❤
♓	Pisces	Sexy affair	❤❤❤

TRADITIONAL ASSOCIATIONS

Colours:
Purple, dark blues

Countries:
Australia, Spain

Tarot Card:
Number 14,
Temperance

Flowers:
Dandelions

Birthstone:
Topaz,. amethyst

Animals:
Horses, stags,
peacocks

Occupations:
Travel
representative's,
Teachers, Lawyers,
Veterinarians

Herbs:
Borage

Trees:
Oak , lime, mulberry

Cities:
Sydney, Avignon,
Stuttgart, Toronto

Food:
Food from around
the world

You love animals, and keeping pets is a rewarding and challenging hobby. Sagittarians are always very drawn to travel, and for some, this wanderlust leads to long sojourns abroad, while others satisfy their appetite with exotic holidays and trips. You love exploring diverse cultures and sampling the various tastes and sensations from around the world.

You need variety, freedom and movement, finding dead-end situations heavy and oppressive. Sagittarians like to be honest and open at all times, and being forced to keep your feelings hidden is a real strain. You do not hold onto the past, preferring instead to look forwards with optimism and hope.

Every once in a while you enjoy a binge of some sort, as you hate having to be careful with money. Sagittarians need to take risks, or otherwise, your energy stagnates.

BELOW *You enjoy the occasional bet from time to time – and you are known as the luckiest of all the signs.*

Capricorn

Capricorns are ambitious, with an instinctual drive to reach the top. The route is carefully planned, and you work steadily to fulfil your personal goals. You are sure-footed, and cling to your vision with tenacity and drive. Once the dizzying heights of success have been achieved, you take little time to relax and enjoy the view, as you once again scan the horizon for new peaks to climb.

Capricorns are serious and disciplined, with a strong need to have their lives organized, and well-thought out. You like to have a tangible, long-term destination, in order to know where you are going and why. You are patient and cautious, possessing a down-to-earth nature that is involved with both the practical and material side of life.

For many Capricorns, a career is all-important, and your self-worth often stems from gaining status and respect in your particular field. This desire to prove yourself means that great hardship can be endured for the sake of achieving your chosen goal. Financial security is a prime concern, and your resources are managed with prudence and wisdom. You obtain real satisfaction from watching the slow-but-inexorable growth of your business affairs.

Capricorns are responsible, with high moral standards and a mature outlook. You are at heart a traditionalist, and prefer sticking to well-worn paths and established social mores. Fear of public embarrassment means that you are reluctant to deviate from the norm. This unwillingness to experiment and take risks can halt the flow of progress in all areas of your life, but you are also blessed with a wry sense of humour, and deep sensuality that revels in earthly delights. You gain happiness from having the courage to listen and respond to the many different levels of your being.

The typical Capricorn man has a well-developed frame with a strong jaw and defined features, and bright, knowing eyes. Beards are common when young, and a serious and slightly grim expression may be worn, which noticeably relaxes with age. You tend to walk with nimble steps, as though picking your way across a stony path.

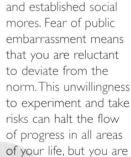

You seem to have a maturity beyond your actual years, and for some Capricorn men, the youthful part of life is a real trial. You feel more comfortable with adults, and relish the chance to get out into the world and take your place alongside them. From an early age, ambitions are uppermost in your mind, and you do not let go until you have gained a secure foothold in your desired career.

Capricorn men are modest and self-effacing, preferring to stay behind the scenes while honours are given elsewhere. Even if your

ABOVE *The more usual though bizarre portrayal of Capricorn is to be seen in the roundel taken from an English Psalter, York, c.1170.*

EXERCISE

Work-obsessed Capricorns can spend far too much time slumped behind a desk, creating a sluggish body and dull, passive mind. To overcome this, try to work out before getting down to paperwork. Many Capricorns have to fight an aversion to regular exercise.

Keep your joints limbered with long walks, jogging and gentle stretching. Yoga will also help you to relax. For more challenging sport, hiking and rock climbing give you a chance to see the beauty of mountains and hills, places where you feel very much at home. Capricorns benefit from being with nature.

work has attained lasting glory, you avoid publicity content instead with inner fulfilment and the recognition of your peers. You have a warm and reserved personality that mellows with age like a fine wine. A secure romance does much to temper your gruff manner, and helps you to overcome emotional isolation. Many of you are prepared to study hard in order to gain recognition and success in the eyes of the world.

Capricorn women tend to have small, well-proportioned bodies with fine bones and classic beauty. Your eyes are sensuous and intriguing. You are conscious of your appearance, and dress with dignity and pride. Like the men, your face reflects sobriety in youth, and lightens up as years go by.

ABOVE *As surefooted as a mountain goat, this rock climber edges upwards with typical Capricorn purpose.*

Capricorns are self-possessed, and you have the determination and focus to succeed. Once your heart and mind have set a course, potential difficulties are brushed aside by your rock-solid focus. Your energy is often geared towards ascending the ladder at work to reach a position of status and respect. You work hard to present an image of stability to the outside world, and disguise whatever troubles you are going through. Capricorn women sometimes encounter quite harsh fates, yet are capable of shouldering heavy burdens without complaining. You have a built-in sense of duty and obligation, and must be careful not to shut out potential happiness by accepting

unnecessary strife. Your personal desires are sacred, and have every right to be fulfiled. A close relationship allows you to open up and receive much-needed love and support.

Capricorn men and women have an essentially conservative approach to fashion. You shy away from unconventionality, preferring instead to go for formal, modest and appropriate outfits. When buying clothes, you are motivated by price, quality and durability, and pay little attention to short-term trends.

PRESENTS

- Quality office accessories
- Weekend at a country inn
- Useful computer software
- Fine goats' cheese
- Mountain holidays
- Status symbols
- Sturdy shoes
- Classy perfumes
- Beautiful books
- Framed family-tree outline or family heirlooms

An austere streak means a few of you will wear clothes until they really wear out, but most Capricorns are anxious to maintain a smart and respectable image. Your thriftiness makes you hunt for a bargain before parting with precious cash, but work clothes are an exception, and you are prepared to spend big in order to make an impression that furthers your burgeoning aims.

At the office, Capricorn women look good in sobre dress suits that have an aura of efficiency and calm. You are drawn to dark tones of grey and brown, with occasional greens lightening the mood. Patent-leather shoes are popular, and executive-type briefcases lend an air of sophistication. For leisure wear, you avoid sloppy, unstylish garments and enjoy relaxing in designer casuals. A romantic evening provides the perfect setting for you to dazzle in a classic suit or little black dress. Jewellery completes the effect.

When choosing a home, Capricorns are guided by their respect for tradition and status. For you, property is a serious investment, and a superb opportunity to increase your social status. Living in the

HEALTH

Capricorns like to work hard, and this can lead to stress-related problems. You thrive on a certain amount of pressure, but have difficulty knowing when to stop. When run down, your weakened immune system makes minor complaints hard to shift, and unreleased tension can prevent a good night's sleep. As most Capricorns possess a very strong constitution, a little moderation usually ensures marvellous levels of health.

The main body parts related to your sign are the knees, teeth, and bones. Advancing years can produce stiffness in the joints, and this is exacerbated by sedentary living or dampness. You are also vulnerable to cavities, and may be a familiar patient in your dentist's surgery. You are advised to take scrupulous care of your teeth.

Capricorns can become very melancholic, with depression gradually seeping into your bones until every day is grey and morose. This can bring about chronic fatigue, and it's important for you to recognize when your spirits are getting low so you can get your life back on an even keel.

Capricorns are very tough, and face serious disease with a stoic fortitude; usually, your endurance wins through in the end.

must be respectable. You prefer conventional furnishings, with subdued colour schemes for the decor. Capricorns enjoy looking after family heirlooms, and these are frequently displayed alongside more recently acquired antiques.

Capricorns feel very relaxed within their domain, and visitors are treated as honoured guests. Once you have invited someone for a meal, you will undoubtedly provide a memorable occasion.

You have excellent money-management skills which enable you to plan far into the future in anticipation of your needs. Saving comes naturally, and you are horrified at the thought of frivolous spending. Sometimes a spartan lifestyle is the result of too much fear, and you hoard your cash for no good reason.

Capricorns are not inclined to take risks, and when it comes to choosing the most appropriate way to invest, you check out expert advice and look

country is appealing, but the rigours of a modern career mean you either reside in a city or suburb.

If it is more economical, you prefer to buy a home of your own, as this seems much wiser to you than wasting money on rent. You have an astute sense for market trends, and will wait until a favourable time to buy. Strong links to your family mean that inherited properties are always cherished.

Capricorns like grand old houses and apartments, with spacious, well-proportioned rooms. If possible, you reside in the best neighbourhoods, and at the very least, the immediate vicinity for steady, long-term gains. You are innately patient, and are very sceptical of get-rich-quick schemes. You are prepared to work exceptionally hard in order to achieve some measure of financial freedom, sometimes enduring harsh conditions while you pave your way to success.

Capricorns are attracted to life insurance and other investment plans that take time to mature. You have a talent for slow empire-building, and over time, may amass a huge fortune. The stock market is a possible source of profit, and many Capricorns show a talent for business, growing into powerful, prominent tycoons.

Leisure is not a priority for industrious Capricorns. Career comes first, and spare hours are often spent boosting its progress. Some people fail to appreciate that you actually enjoy working hard, and can find it difficult to get involved in activities that to you, seem like wasting time.

When your job is going well, you are more inclined to indulge in relaxing pursuits. Capricorns have a reserved, reflective psyche, and you like to unwind with a thought-provoking book. Museums satisfy an interest in the past, and you can become something of an amateur historian.

You are attracted to formal study and training that have useful qualifications, and enjoy socializing in

		How Capricorn finds:	At a glance
♈	Aries	Childish	❤❤
♉	Taurus	Deep love	❤❤❤❤❤
♊	Gemini	Keep walking!	❤
♋	Cancer	Perfect partners	❤❤❤❤❤
♌	Leo	Surprisingly possible	❤❤❤
♍	Virgo	The earth moves	❤❤❤❤❤
♎	Libra	Forget it	❤❤
♏	Scorpio	Intense but good	❤❤❤❤
♐	Sagittarius	Restless non-event	❤
♑	Capricorn	Mountain-top delight	❤❤❤❤❤
♒	Aquarius	Complementary	❤❤❤
♓	Pisces	Sublime romance	❤❤❤❤❤

academic settings. Evening classes meet your creative needs, and you have a penchant for pottery and art. Many Capricorns are home-maintenance enthusiasts, as you possess both practical hands and a desire to economize. Friends are very important and you make every effort to stay in touch. You celebrate your work triumphs in style, usually inviting everyone to toast your success.

You have a strong sense of modesty, and dislike being thrust into the limelight, especially if you are on unfamiliar ground. Capricorns respect tradition and the status quo, and feel threatened by radical, anarchistic views. New ideas can at first be rejected on principle.

You conduct yourself with dignity, anxious to avoid any public humiliation. Your personal feelings are private, and not for public knowledge. Capricorns need to feel rooted to the past, and will delight in passing on something worthwhile to future generations.

TRADITIONAL ASSOCIATIONS

Colours:
Shades of grey and brown

Countries:
India, Afghanistan

Tarot Card:
Number 15, the Devil

Flowers:
Hellebore

Birthstone:
Jet, onyx

Animals:
Goats, bears, bats

Occupations:
Antique dealers, Real estate agents, Systems analysts, Archaeologists

Herbs:
Comfrey

Trees:
Yew, pine

Cities:
Brussels, Delhi, Oxford

Food:
Meat and salted nuts

Aquarius

Aquarians have a strong independent spirit that longs to break free
from the restrictions imposed by conventional ideas. You are idealistic
and innovative, replacing old and outdated thinking with fresh
perspectives. Strongly drawn towards humanitarian issues, you
experiment to discover your true identity.

Aquarians are nonconformists, and are not afraid to break away from convention. You are determined to follow your principles, even if this means shunning considered opinion and forging ahead on your own. Rebelling against the crowd gives you something to fight, and you possess a deep-rooted need to reform the status quo.

You explore many visionary concepts, which only time may judge. Some are later dismissed as mere eccentricity while a few will pre-empt future trends with an illuminating flash of genius. Aquarians obtain a perverse satisfaction in rejecting established values, even when these have inherent worth. With maturity, you learn to separate the wheat from the chaff, and understand changing cycles in light of history.

In your search for utopia, you are prepared to go it alone. This contradiction makes personal relationships a challenge, and your inner detachment struggles with emotional commitment. Part of you desperately wants to be close, but you also want to stay free. It is not always easy to reconcile these opposing points of view, and many Aquarians have to adjust to living with compromise. You have a global consciousness, and appreciate each culture for what it has to offer. Aquarians vehemently oppose prejudice, and you are deeply stirred by social injustice and oppression. This concern with humanity allows you to recognize that the individual is responsible for the whole.

The Aquarian man tends to be fairly tall, with lithe limbs and strong bones. You often appear deep in thought, and when your interest is aroused, your eyes sparkle and your brows rise. You walk quickly unless you are deep in thought, when your steps can be irregular, and your head is slightly lowered.

Aquarians must express their originality and you are attracted to experiences and concepts that help you to solidify your sense of self. By being prepared to leave tradition behind, you find out what you really believe in, and how to utilize your unique perceptions.

You are fascinated by alternative

ABOVE *You love the expansiveness of the mountains, and the sense of true freedom this inspires in you.*

ways of living, and how modern technology can be used to heal the planet. Aquarians have a scientific bent, and you combine this with a sharp intuition to reason and probe new frontiers of thought. Your emotions may be sublimated by logic, and your cool persona can make you appear to be rather offhand. But once you find your mission, life has tremendous focus and clarity.

For Aquarian men, a loving union is the ultimate test, and provides you with the opportunity to reveal your soul.

The typical Aquarian woman has a large bone structure and a well-proportioned face. You have clear, lively eyes that dart back and forth, with a fresh complexion and an open disposition. If you become excited, your arms move frantically, and your whole body takes on an electric presence.

Aquarians have an essentially unpredictable nature. Your feelings are prone to change without warning, which can cause confusion. At times

EXERCISE

Modest amounts of walking, swimming and cycling do much to keep your blood flowing and your joints supple. If you pick a fun activity that is easy to integrate into your lifestyle, the transformation to better fitness will be relatively painless!

Aquarians often enjoy skiing, as you relish good clean air and the healthful environment of the mountains.

Dancing gives you the chance to express yourself physically, and Aquarians have a good sense of rhythm and a natural ease with sound. To stretch both body and mind, the eastern disciplines of aikido and t'ai chi give you insight into the nature of energy.

ABOVE *Aquarians are great humanitarians, and are often drawn to professions where they care for others.*

discovered how to live by your principles. You long to find a partner who can accept your independence and understand your profound emotional shifts.

Aquarians have an individualistic approach to fashion, and you resist slavishly pursuing current trends, unless they really catch your eye. You can be quite experimental with your choice of clothes, and are attracted to styles that have originality and flair. Some

you yearn for close and intimate company; then, out of the blue, a sense of claustrophobia descends, and you withdraw to seek solace alone.

As life progresses, you are able to stay centred while the pendulum swings, and this brings you growing confidence and peace. Aquarian women are strongly attuned to the earth and to people, and you enjoy being involved with small and large communities, often supporting groups that aim to improve others' lives. Aquarian women must follow the dictates of their conscience, and you will only be happy when you have

PRESENTS

- Unusual gifts
- Computer software and electronic gizmos
- New Age books
- Alternative medicines
- Crystals and stones
- Organic foods and wines
- Silk and satin clothes
- Natural sandals
- Unusual flowers
- Tickets for futuristic shows or exhibitions

Aquarians are very daring and happily flirt with outrageous, avant-garde designs, but most of you are more modest, limiting yourself to an audacious use of colour.

You are often seduced by images that spring from social movements. These outfits embody the ideas of the time, and you sometimes cling to these styles, even if they have ceased to be relevant – Aquarians can be extremely rigid in this way. Both sexes recoil from faceless conformity and if forced to wear a uniform as part of your work, you like to wear accessories to maintain your individuality.

Women have a vivid sense of colour, and are especially drawn to vibrant turquoise blues and greens. Purple is also popular. You prefer jobs that allow freedom of expression, and you tend to select garments that are comfortable and harmonize with your moods. Smooth, silky textures are favoured, and when dressing up, you exude glamour.

Aquarian men are less eccentric dressers, but still display a marked defiance of convention. You feel relaxed in casuals, and feel much more at ease in these, whatever the demands of the situation.

HEALTH

Your hectic lifestyle may preclude sufficient exercise to ensure good health. Aquarians have intense minds that seek plenty of stimulation, but you are not always so in tune with your body's needs. Lack of movement on a daily basis constricts energy and hinders the circulatory system. In winter, numbness in the hands and feet can develop into swelling if not kept in check. In extreme instances, you have difficulty adjusting to both hot and cold weather. A sensible physical regime ensures that you are able to maintain your internal equilibrium.

The ankles are linked to the sign of Aquarius, and are prone to twists and sprains. You should be extra careful when playing sports, and make an effort to wear appropriate shoes. You are resilient, and take most minor complaints in your stride. On the rare occasions that serious disease penetrates your defences, you may be opposed to conventional medicine, preferring instead to trust your recovery to alternative treatments.

These usually prove remarkably effective, and seem to suit your particular constitution. Aquarians are also subject to sudden and inexplicable ills that quickly vanish without a trace.

LEFT *Aquarius is depicted in a sixteenth century Turkish treatise on astrology as drawing water from a well. Eastern and western artistic conventions frequently differ in presentation even when dealing with similar ideas or symbols.*

You hold no allegiance to a particular location, and appreciate the merits of both the country and the city. Aquarians prefer their residence to be spacious and airy, with plenty of natural light. You are fastidious about clutter, as this imbues a feeling of constriction. The general ambience you create is cool and fresh, with striking, imaginative colours. Finances permitting, you indulge a passion for gadgets and technology to create an up-to-date and perhaps space-age abode. The sparse use of furniture complements the overall mood.

As the years go by, it becomes increasingly important for you to have a home of your own. Because of your principles, this can be hard to admit.

Aquarians are not motivated by a desire to make vast fortunes. If one of your brilliant ideas catches on, riches may indeed result, but you are more concerned with communicating your vision, and take little comfort from material gain. Whatever you do must find accord with your altruistic stance. Aquarians are strongly advised to seek expert advice before trying to get one of their more radical or eccentric schemes off the ground. This will avoid many potential pitfalls and disasters.

Your experimental lifestyles can produce some unusual homes. Aquarians are often interested in sharing property with others, and for some time you may avoid living alone. It makes you feel secure to be part of a group, and you enjoy the sense of collective responsibility. Some idealistic Aquarians live in bohemian New Age communes, and are great believers in housing cooperatives. You are idealistic, and happy to help out friends who have nowhere to stay.

While you are so absorbed with other areas of your life, your finances may be neglected. You dislike being hemmed in by a lack of cash, so you usually make an effort to be self-sufficient. Aquarians are resourceful, and if pushed, you dig up some fairly unorthodox ways to earn money. The harsh reality of debt eventually teaches you to curb your extravagant tendencies. Aquarians are not greedy, and many keep their savings in a basic account. Ethical investments appeal, as you like to know where your money is going and what it will be used for. Whatever your level of wealth, this is generously shared with family and friends.

The strong humanitarian side of the Aquarian nature shows itself in many practical ways, and you enjoy making donations to favourite charities.

Aquarians like to pursue eclectic interests in their leisure time. You enjoy studying, and can find New Age topics very inspiring. One aspect of this field may grow into a consuming hobby, or possibly a future career. Aquarians are always receptive to ideas on the cutting edge of science and culture.

Your social circle is likely to consist of unusual individuals, united by their free-thinking and unconventional approach to life. To an outsider, this assortment may appear disparate. Thought-provoking plays and movies

	How Aquarius finds:		At a glance
♈	Aries	Exciting love	♥♥♥♥
♉	Taurus	Uninspiring	♥♥♥
♊	Gemini	Heaven!	♥♥♥♥♥
♋	Cancer	Disastrous	♥
♌	Leo	Stubborn partners	♥♥♥
♍	Virgo	You must be kidding!	♥
♎	Libra	Fresh 'n' sweet	♥♥♥♥♥
♏	Scorpio	Interesting...	♥♥♥
♐	Sagittarius	Tops for passion	♥♥♥♥♥
♑	Capricorn	Surprisingly possible	♥♥♥
♒	Aquarius	True soul-mates	♥♥♥♥♥
♓	Pisces	Magnetic affair	♥♥♥

appeal, especially if they concern issues close to your heart. You are interested in parties, but your capricious moods mean it's hard to predict whether you will actually turn up!

Aquarians appreciate shared company, but you are also reluctant to pin yourself down with too many commitments. Sometimes you refuse an invitation purely to keep your options open. You often decide to visit a friend on a whim, and likewise are happy for people to come over on short notice.

Aquarians dislike being forced to conform – you are intrigued by the concept of a global village. If you really feel stifled, you behave rebelliously. You have a soft spot for futuristic technology, and are often among the first to acquire the latest executive toy.

Aquarians hate getting stuck in a rut, and when this happens, you are open to being freed by sudden and exciting events. You enjoy persuading others to change their minds, but are yourself somewhat inflexible.

Aquarians are usually pacifists, and you recoil from the thought of violence.

LEFT *Aquarians are interested in exploring alternative political ideologies, cultures and religions.*

Pisces

Dreamy and sensitive, Pisceans are blessed with deep intuition and a wealth of emotion. You live in the world of feelings, and your mutable nature ebbs and flows in tune with an inner tide. Your imagination is so strong that at times it merges reality with fantasy. Pisceans need time to understand the true calling of their souls

Pisceans are kind and compassionate, with an empathy for your fellow human beings that makes it hard for you not to care even when it interferes with your own life.

You are very open, and you sometimes feel like an emotional sponge, absorbing both positive and negative energy from those around you. This lack of boundaries may leave you feeling drained, and to recharge your delicate psyche, it is essential to rest a while in a tranquil, private setting. Pisceans are vulnerable to losing their identity by pouring themselves into other people. Like a river seeking the sea, you were born with an instinct to transcend yourself through merging with something greater.

This desire can take you across an ocean of experience from the divinity of mystical union to the degradation of alcoholic despair. Pisceans are capable of both these extremes as well as every shore that lies between.

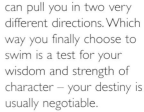

You are often unsure about how you feel, and the resulting ambivalence can pull you in two very different directions. Which way you finally choose to swim is a test for your wisdom and strength of character – your destiny is usually negotiable.

On occasions your sensitivity may make life painful and difficult. You may be tempted to escape, but by facing these challenges courageously, you can trawl up treasures from the deep. Pisceans are romantic, creative and full of love, with a potential for great happiness and lasting joy.

The average Piscean man has a slightly bulbous head, with eyes that are set well back, seeming to gaze at distant horizons. Your shoulders are prominent, and you walk a bit like a sailor, with a pronounced rolling gait. Your eyebrows are often thick, and your face is very mutable, conveying a variety of expressions that change with your mood.

You are a natural romantic, determined to pursue as many of your dreams as possible. The amazing Piscean imagination is able to achieve the fantastic and unbelievable, but occasionally you discover that you are in fact only chasing pipe dreams. A refusal to acknowledge reality even when it is obvious, can produce little more than empty musing.

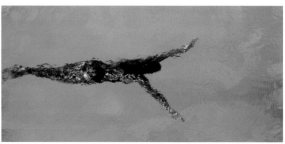

ABOVE *You love floating gently and merging with the water that surrounds you.*

EXERCISE

Pisceans love water, and swimming is a natural choice for exercise that tones the body and peacefully releases tension. You sometimes find crowded, noisy environments insufferable, and would rather go for a quiet, solitary walk, preferably in the woods or country.

Mental relaxation is vital, and yoga offers gentle stretching that soothes your mind. With regular practice, you may achieve new levels of emotional balance, and for many Pisceans, yoga is the perfect antidote to stress. Ballet and dance appeal to your romantic nature, and you find the music uplifting.

The Piscean man is very emotional, and you are more sensitive than you care to admit. You employ your formidable intuition to dodge problems, rather than tackling them head on. This softness of approach is one of your greatest assets, and allows you to elude danger and maximize opportunity.

Pisceans like to have romance and intrigue in their lives, and when involved in a good relationship, you view life through rose-tinted glasses. Your heart longs for such a loving union.

The typical Piscean woman is slim when younger, but tends to hold water and put on weight with age. You have a moon-shaped face, with mysterious eyes and an alluring smile. After a hard day you look exhausted, and any current worries show up in your expression. When relaxed, you are radiant and serene.

Piscean women have nebulous feelings that produce confusing extremes of elation and disappointment. You are sometimes at the mercy of these emotions, which threaten to engulf your fragile sense of self. Experience teaches you that by surrendering to the flow of your watery nature, you survive intact, with renewed faith.

It is vital that you should share your emotional life by talking with friends, releasing tears if required. You are very loving and considerate, finding it hard to refuse if someone asks for help. You are susceptible to outside influences, and have difficulty seeing yourself in a positive light. Maturity brings increased perspective and confidence.

Piscean women have a soft, vulnerable image that belies their inner fortitude. You yearn for a strong, supportive partner who appreciates the depth of your love and also has the sensitivity to respond.

PRESENTS

- Champagne
- Romantic books/music
- Beach holiday
- Seafood
- Mystical gifts
- Paintings
- Belgian chocolates
- Aquarium
- Flowers
- Glamourous night out

BELOW *Pisceans are born romantics and you love sharing intimate times with your nearest and dearest.*

HEALTH

Pisceans' sensitive constitution means your health is directly influenced by how you are feeling. When you are emotionally drained, you are subject to a variety of minor ills that are often psychosomatic. It is important to listen to your subconscious, as you can gain useful insight into which situations to avoid.

With more serious illness, you tend to give in to it, letting it wash over you until it finally recedes. For a Piscean, this is the quickest route to recovery. Friends and family support you, and your fighting spirit is stimulated by love. When suffering from severe stress, some Pisceans are prone to seek relief through alcohol and drugs. Your inclination towards addiction should make you extremely moderate when indulging in social pleasures.

The feet are the main body part relating to Pisces, and you may suffer from corns, warts, bunions, and swelling. It is imperative that you wear comfortable, roomy shoes with good support. In winter, a gentle foot massage with a stimulating oil can enhance circulation and help keep your feet in good condition.

Pisceans have a quiet magnetism that adds a glamourous touch to the most humble outfits. Your clothes tend to reflect how things are going in your life, and when times are hard or you are disorganized, you may lack the energy to take care of your appearance. However, you still exude charm even when you are sloppy.

Pisceans are drawn to shimmering colours, evocative textures, and romantic images far removed from mundane drabness. You gladly spend money to achieve your desired look, and your wardrobe is a testimony to your ever-changing lifestyle and nature.

At work, women wear sensible, but feminine, skirts and dresses. You are well aware of your attractiveness to the opposite sex, and use this in many subtle ways. Soft, comfortable casuals are your favourite choice for hanging around, and you enjoy relaxing without make-up. For a special night out, you emulate Cinderella at the ball, resplendent in a beautiful, magical dress, with matching shoes and subtle perfume to evoke passion and intrigue.

Piscean men may feel slightly awkward in a suit, as you are generally more at ease in casual clothes with fluid, stylish lines. You love wearing the sea colours, and for a special dinner or night out, will dazzle with astute grooming and romantic panache.

The Piscean abode provides a safe harbour from the harsh environment of the outside world. Privacy and

ABOVE *Pisces is commonly represented as two fish swimming in opposite directions, their mouths joined by a line. The latter owes its existence to a string of stars which joins the groups that form the fish.*

tranquillity are absolutely vital, and give you a chance to unwind and release any built-up stress. Pisceans love to live by water, and you really appreciate the soothing beauty of the sea. Cities are exciting, but the sheer mass of humanity can tax your *joie de vivre*.

Even if you live in a concrete jungle, your apartment's interior will have a gentle, relaxing atmosphere. When choosing somewhere to live, you are guided by gut feelings, and can easily visualize its appearance after decorating and furnishing.

Pisceans like rich colours and fabrics that create a full-bodied, emotive mood. Your attachment to accumulated possessions means this flotsam and jetsam can create some interesting scenery. You give rooms real character when you adorn them with personal items, paintings and houseplants.

The general impression is warm and welcoming, though sometimes a little cluttered. Pisceans are sensitive hosts, and always make guests feel relaxed and at home.

Pisceans' unworldly streak may make it hard for you to get to grips with personal finance. You must make a real effort to focus on annoying details in order to keep your head above water; some careless Pisceans lurch from one financial disaster to another.

You are generous in the extreme, and can be easily moved by a sob story. Make sure your own needs are well taken care of before you start administering to others. You enjoy spending funds to have a fulfiling life; because you are not very materialistic; following your heart is more important than acquiring riches. Provided you have enough to live comfortably, you are generally quite content.

Some Pisceans are seduced by the glamour of wealth, and may be exploited by unscrupulous people, who talk you into making dubious investments. Your fertile imagination can lead you astray, so before actually parting with any hard cash, you should seek the advice of a reputable expert. Pisceans benefit from learning to save, and thus creating a useful buffer against any future adversity

Your leisure hours are very precious, as you often find day-to-day existence a strain. When really tired, many Pisceans enjoy curling up with a good book or a long session in front of the TV. It is not unusual for you to take a refreshing nap, and you love the feeling of having absolutely nothing to do.

Pisceans are artistically inclined. Your superb imagination can find expression through painting, music and writing. Fantasy and myth are popular themes for you to explore and you may enjoy studying these in an evening class or group. You love your many friends dearly, and relish the time you are able to spend together. Intimate dinners in, and colourful nights out, give you a chance to catch up on the latest gossip and share your life with others. With company, it is even harder for you to resist indulging your sweet tooth and passion for wine!

	How Pisces finds:		At a glance
♈	Aries	Impulsive and forceful	❤❤
♉	Taurus	Secure loving	❤❤❤❤
♊	Gemini	Superficial	❤
♋	Cancer	Sweet 'n' deep	❤❤❤❤❤
♌	Leo	Short-term fizzler	❤❤❤
♍	Virgo	Pragmatic partner	❤❤❤❤
♎	Libra	Once in a while	❤❤❤
♏	Scorpio	Yes!.	❤❤❤❤❤
♐	Sagittarius	Steamy affair	❤❤❤
♑	Capricorn	Rock-solid lover	❤❤❤❤❤
♒	Aquarius	Unstable attraction	❤❤
♓	Pisces	Ultimate romance	❤❤❤❤❤

For a big night out, you like movies, theatre, and glamourous, intriguing parties – Pisceans need romance and magic in all they do.

Pisceans love walking by the sea at sunset, allowing their thoughts to drift with the tide. Sometimes your spirit cries out for nature, and you simply have to get out of the city for a short break in more peaceful surroundings. If you feel life is drab and grey, every once in a while you need to make a temporary escape.

Being forced to be logical and rational can make you depressed. Pisceans are creatures of emotion, and you don't like feeling too cut off and detached. You are a very private person, and find it difficult to cope with situations requiring exposure.

TRADITIONAL ASSOCIATIONS

Colours:
Sea greens, violet

Tarot Card:
Number 18, the Moon

Flowers:
Iris

Birthstone:
Pearl, moonstone

Animals:
Fish, dolphins

Occupations:
Dancers, Healers, Musicians, Artists, Psychics

Herbs:
Evening Primrose

Trees:
Willow, hazel

Cities:
Lisbon, Seville, Venice

Food:
Fruit, Vegetables with a high water content

LEFT *Pisceans have rich and creative imaginations, and this is often reflected in the way you design and furnish your home.*

Tarot

The tarot resembles an enlarged pack of playing cards.
In the standard tarot pack are 78 cards (as compared to
52 in a normal British or American pack of playing cards).
Most of the extra cards are the trumps or Major Arcana.
There are 22 of these, numbered 1 to 21, together with the
Fool (not numbered but often thought of as number 0).
The rest of the pack (the Minor Arcana) consists of four
suites: swords, wands (sometimes known as rods, sceptres,
staves or batons), cups and pentacles (also called coins
or discs). Each suit has cards numbered familiarly
from 1 to 10 and four court cards, the king,
the queen, the knight and the page.
Many different origins have been claimed for the tarot.
It might be based on an ancient Egyptian book;
it might be Indian, connected with a forerunner of the
game of chess; it might have originally been Arabic,
perhaps brought to Europe by returning crusaders; it might
have travelled west from Asia to Europe with the movement
of wandering gypsies. In fact, nobody knows for sure.

MODERN-DAY TAROT

Over the last 15 years the tarot has been dramatically popularized. From being a scarce and rather esoteric fortune-telling device used by specialists and issued in a few packs with traditional designs, the tarot has become big business in the games and *objet d'art* markets. Dozens and dozens of newly designed packs have been marketed. Some have been showcases for the work of one or more artists. The surrealist, Salvador Dali illustrated a richly symbolic pack, using collage, as one of his last major works. Some have taken symbols from different mythological or cultural backgrounds, so that there are Celtic and Greek myth packs, a Japanese pack and an Amer-indian pack. Others portray invented worlds, fantasy settings or futures. In addition, a few very early packs have been issued in restored form. Most of these packs are very beautiful, well worth seeing and eminently collectable. Many such packs are purchased and never used for fortune telling.

BELOW *Modern-day tarot has become big business with many newly designed packs being marketed and collected, ranging from Celtic and Greek myth packs to invented worlds, fantasy settings or futures.*

The Major Arcana

The 22 cards of the Major Arcana ('Greater Secrets') are also known as the Trumps or Triumphs, and are sometimes referred to by the French *atouts* or the Italian *atutti* or *trionfi*. These are the cards containing strong prototypal symbols and meanings.

THE FOOL: 0

THE FOOL

This is the only unnumbered card of the Major Arcana. It is generally regarded as card number 0, and is placed first. It has evolved into the joker of the present-day British and American pack of playing cards. A complex card, standing for many things one should avoid, including foolishness, thoughtlessness, recklessness; a lack of discipline or restraint; excessive behaviour, obsession or infatuation. It also stands for lightheartedness and pleasure. It is a warning to make the right choice in a vital matter rather than taking an easy way out.

R a faulty choice or a lack of decision.

THE MAGICIAN

THE MAGICIAN: I

A creative card; power, skill and trickery; determination to finish projects and to use one's own talents well.

R lack of will; misuse of power; hesitation; ineptitude.

R indicates a reversed card (top to bottom).

THE HIGH PRIESTESS: 2

Wisdom and understanding; intuition; teaching; mystery, something hidden; serenity and an avoidance of emotional relationships.

R superficiality, ignorance and poor judgement.

THE EMPRESS: 3

Traditional 'female' accomplishments, such as marriage, children, motivating others.

R inaction, domestic problems and resources wasted.

THE EMPEROR: 4

Traditional 'male' success: power over others, leadership, wealth, strength, fatherhood; intelligence dominating emotion.

R immaturity, lack of strength and lack of control.

THE HIEROPHANT (HIGH PRIEST): 5

Spiritual power, ritual; kind and merciful; conventional and conformist, even unwilling to change. Teacher or advisor.

R unconventional, vulnerable, gullible.

THE LOVERS 6

The conflict or choice between flesh and spirit. Love relationships, romance, feelings; harmony and perfection.

R wrong choice, interference, break-up of relationship.

THE CHARIOT 7

A contradictory card concerned with change and movement. Troubles and turmoil; problems overcome, success; progress; a journey.

R sudden collapse, defeat, failure.

JUSTICE 8

Justice, balance, reasonableness; the outcome will be fair; temptation is recognized and evil avoided.

R injustice, the abuse of power, bigotry, misjudgement.

THE HERMIT 9

Wisdom, prudence; a movement towards spiritual goals. Also desertion, annulment, a person alone.

R foolishness, a refusal to stop and think; immaturity.

THE WHEEL OF FORTUNE 10

Unexpected good fortune; completion or solution; outcome for good or bad depending on adjacent cards; change and advancement.

R bad luck, decline, interruption.

STRENGTH 11

Adversity is overcome by courage, strength, fortitude; physical ability; conquest of peril; love triumphs over hate.

R weakness; obstacles not surmounted; lack of faith.

THE HANGED MAN 12

Change; decisions suspended for a while; sacrifice without immediate reward; rebirth and improvement coming.

R rigid refusal to sacrifice oneself; lack of effort.

DEATH 13

Unexpected change, transformation; endings and beginnings for better or worse; illness; spiritual rebirth; progress from setbacks.

R stagnation; destruction without renewal.

TEMPERANCE 14

A fortunate card exhorting moderation; patience and frugality; harmony between material and spiritual things.

R lack of harmony; arguments, conflicts and hostilities.

THE DEVIL 15

Ominous events, including downfall, failure, subservience and bad influences; even death and disasters. Sexual temptation.

R respite, release, spiritual enlightment.

THE TOWER 16

Sudden and complete change. Everything is broken down, severed, disrupted, lost; but rebuilding can take place.

R continuing in a rut, imprisonment (of any kind).

THE STAR 17

A fortunate card bringing bright prospects, hope, new opportunities, successful results from previous hard work.

R lack of opportunity or success; hopes dashed; bad luck.

THE MOON 18

Beware of the trickery of others and deceptive circumstances; errors are likely; friends are false. An irritational card.

R small problems, deceptions or mistakes are overcome.

THE SUN 19

Illumination, accomplishment; contentment from success, love, a happy marriage and simple everyday things.

R loneliness, failure, hopes dashed, broken relationships.

147

JUDGEMENT 20

The weighing-up process of the Day of Judgement; spiritual development or rejuvenation. Review your conduct and atone if necessary.

R regrets, delays, indecision.

THE WORLD 21

Change in the sense of completion; a triumphal result; goals achieved; the cycle ends to begin again; a very favourable card.

R ultimate failure; lack of completion.

Tarot-reading Techniques

Very little of the fine detail of tarot divination is standard. There are many methods of operating and quite a number of different arrangements of the spread, using as few as seven cards (the Seven-Card Spread) or as many as 54 cards (the Royal Spread). The most commonly used today in Britain and America is the Celtic Method, a ten-card spread, which may be performed either from the whole pack or using just the Major Arcana.

Divination with the tarot consists of the diviner spreading (the term for laying out, face up) a certain number of cards and interpreting their meanings. This is normally done in an attempt to answer a question or solve a problem put by the subject (or questioner), which may be voiced or not, as the subject wishes.

It is important to understand that tarot divination is not simply a mechanical procedure of shuffling cards, laying a few out and reading their meanings from a book. There is a spiritual side to it, without which no accurate and helpful reading can be made.

The surroundings should be quiet and conducive to concentration. Probably the diviner and the subject will be alone together in a room, although public readings are occasionally given. The diviner must ensure that he or she is in the right mood for the reading and the subject must have some kind of question or problem in mind.

First (a step sometimes omitted) the diviner removes a court card from the pack to represent the subject. This is a wand if the subject has fair hair and blue

eyes, a cup for light brown hair and pale eyes, a sword for dark brown hair and brown eyes and a pentacle for black hair and dark eyes. For a man as subject, the king of the suit is selected, for a woman the queen, for a young man the knight and for a young woman or child the page. The card, known as the significator, is placed face up on the table in front of the subject.

Then the diviner asks the subject to shuffle the pack. In fact, most diviners dislike anyone else handling their pack (often kept carefully wrapped in black silk and boxed to protect its vibrations) so the diviner may ask the subject only to cut the pack or perhaps just to place his or her hands on the pack for a moment while thinking about the question.

After shuffling, the pack is cut into three face-downward piles (usually by the subject) then picked up by the diviner. The top card is turned over and laid (face up) on top of the significator, covering it completely. The second card is turned over and laid across it. The next eight cards are turned over and laid down strictly in order to form a cross and then a line beside it.

WHAT THE CARDS SIGNIFY

Each of these cards stand for some aspect of the subject's life and situation.

Card 1 the present situation and general atmosphere.

Card 2 the forces in opposition, obstacles.

Card 3 the subject's hopes or goals.

Card 4 distant past events or influences on which the present problem is based.

Card 5 recent events, just past or still passing.

Card 6 future influences.

Sometimes the diviner reads these six cards before turning over the next four.

Card 7 the subject's present attitude or position regarding the problem.

Card 8 those factors surrounding the subject which may be influential.

Card 9 the subject's inner feelings on the problem.

Card 10 the outcome.

If it should happen that more than half the cards are reversed (which radically alters their meaning), the reading cannot be trusted and these reversed cards must be turned upright.

Then the diviner speaks the reading aloud, interpreting each card for its personal symbolism and position.

Sometimes the answer ignores the question asked and penetrates to the heart of the real problem the subject has.

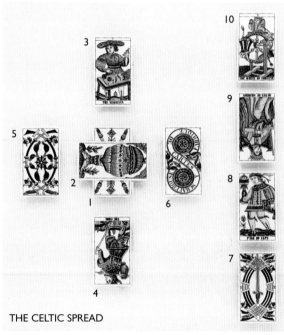

THE CELTIC SPREAD

If the tenth card proves to be weak and unhelpful, a second reading may be done at once using that tenth card as the significator. The pack is shuffled, cut and laid out as before.

A TAROT READING INTERPRETED

The significator was the King of Cups. The question asked was whether the questioner should persevere in his current job or try to find something different. The cards came out as follows:

1 Two of Wands (present position): uncertainty; great potential with some sadness indicated.

2 Ace of Cups (immediate influences): good, on the questioner's side at present.

3 The Magician (hopes): self-confidence will provide the ability to succeed.

4 The Fool reversed (past influences): past decisions were foolish.

5 Two of Swords (influences still passing): the present is a peaceful hiatus in a discordant situation.

6 Two of Pentacles reversed (near-future influences): conflict and an irreconcilable situation.

7 Seven of Swords (questioner's attitude): mixed.

8 Page of Cups (environment, family and friends): help from a younger person, or the birth of an idea.

9 Queen of Swords reversed (hopes and fears): a bad female influence; negative feelings.

10 The Wheel of Fortune (outcome): constant change.

To summarize, this is a strong but mixed reading. It suggests that there are no magical solutions, but that if the questioner believes in himself and sticks at his current job he may do well, being helped by somebody else. Conflicts and changes are an almost inevitable part of life; they need to be accepted and coped with.

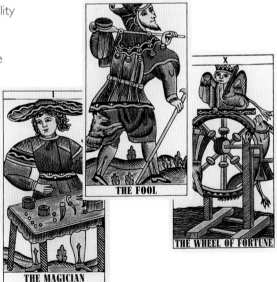

THE FOOL

THE MAGICIAN

THE WHEEL OF FORTUNE

The Minor Arcana

The Minor Arcana consists of 56 cards of four suites: swords, wands (sometimes known as rods, sceptres, staves or batons), cups and pentacles (also called coins or discs). Each suit is numbered familiarly from I to 10 and four court cards, the king, queen, knight and page.

WANDS

King an honest, mature person. Noble, loyal, conscientious, generally married.
R severity. Advice to be taken.

Queen a sympathetic person. Loving, chaste, friendly. Business success.
R economical. jeaousy or deceit.

Knight departure, a journey into the unknown. A young man creating rivalry.
R discord, change, conflict.

Page a faithful young person. An envoy or messenger. Consistent, stable.
R badness, indecision, reluctance.

Ten excessive pressure; power used selfishly; problem soon solved.
R difficulties. treachery, deceit.

Nine strength to face unexpected problems. Readiness.
R obstacles, adversity.

Eight sudden progress, haste, perhaps a journey. Arrows of love.
R jealousy, dispute, disharmony, quarrels.

Seven success over adversity through persistence.
R anxiety, embarrassment, confusion.

Six triumph, gain, advancement, good news.
R indefinite delay, fear, vulnerability.

Five struggle, stiff competition; some hope of general improvement.
R complications, frustrations and contradictions.

Four romance, harmony, prosperity, peace.
R the same.

Three practical help in business; enterprise; strength.
R beware of help. Treachery.

Two mature ruler; boldness; success.
R sadness. Troubles, misfortune.

One beginnings in the widest sense. Fortune.
R false start, decadence.

CUPS

King a professional or business person, generous, responsible.
   R deceit and loss. Artistic temperament, unreliability.

Queen a good wife and mother, intuitive, practical; a visionary.
   R a good woman but inconsistent, untrustworthy, deceitful.

Knight an invitation; advance or change; an intelligent messenger.
   R a subtle, sly, untrustworthy, deceitful person.

Page a helpful, artistic young person; can be a birth or a new idea.
   R obstacles, problems, deviation, distraction

Ten love, friendship, happiness, in home life; success
   R loss of friendship or harmony; strife

Nine material success; good health; spiritual well-being.
   R imperfections, mistakes.

Eight abandonment, withdrawal; decline of something minor.

R joy, feasting, celebration; material success.

Seven too much daydreaming and wishful thinking; little achievement.
   R determination; virtual success.

Six memories, the past, vanished things; change or a desire for it.
   R living in the past; new opportunities

Five loss (not total), regret; hollow friendship or marriage.
   R hope, expectations; promise fulfiled; an old friend returns.

Four discontent, boredom; hesitation despite desire for change.
   R new relationships, possibilites, new beginnings.

Three successful resolution; conclusions; healing
   R excessive physical pleasure

Two love, a new friendship or relationship. Passion; harmony.
   R false love or friendship; disharmony; divorce.

One abundance, joy, happiness; spiritual fulfilment.
   R change, instability

SWORDS

King a powerful professional man, wise and full of ideas.
   R cruelty; some evil brilliance.

Queen a widow, sterile and sad, but perceptive and quick-witted.
   R prudish, narrow-minded.

Knight an active young man; adjacent cards show outcome.
   R extravagance, indiscretion.

Page a perceptive young person; spying, agility; good or evil.
   R unspoken danger; illness.

Ten ruin, trouble, pain, sadness, though not death.
   R temporary benefit or profit.

Nine indecision; failure and desolation; anxiety.
   R doubt and suspicion; imprisonment or confinement.

Eight crisis, conflict; difficulty in escaping.
   R past treachery; difficulties.

Seven plans; uncertainty; potential failure.
   R good advice or instruction.

Six a journey, perhaps by water; success; resolution of difficulties.
   R no solution.

Five physical conquest, or a threat of defeat and dishonour.
   R uncertainly, weakness.

Four respite, recuperation; exile or solitude.
   R activity; economy and care.

Three separation, sorrow, absence, delay.
   R distraction, disorder, confusion.

Two stalemate through balanced forces; harmony; truce.
   R falsehood, release.

One great force or hatred; excess; fertility.
   R self-destruction from extremes.

PENTACLES

King an intelligent and successful person, strong character; may be leader.
   R corruption, perversity, dissipation, intoxication.

Queen prosperity, opulence, security; a rich but generous person.
   R suspicion, neglect, mistrust.

Knight a reliable and methodical young man; hard working and patient.
   R idleness, stagnation, laziness, carelessness.

Page a careful and diligent young person; scholarship; new idea sought.
   R dissipation and rebellion.

Ten a prosperous lineage; gain; family matters; home.
   R loss of money or family reputation.

Nine something accomplished; material or financial security; prudence.
   R danger; a threat to safety or possessions.

Eight an apprenticeship; skill; a future commission.
   R ambition lacking; failure.

Seven business growth via hard work; success; barter
   R anxiety and impatience, especially over money.

Six generosity: success shared.
   R greed, selfishness, envy.

Five poverty, loneliness; spiritual or emotional loss..
   R reversal of bad fortune; marriage problems.

Four obsessed with material. wealth, miserly.
   R setbacks, obstacles, loss.

Three mastery of a skill in business or art, mobility.
   R lack of skill and care; pettiness.

Two problems with new projects; agility needed; some harmony.
   R enjoyment simulated; written messages.

One perfection, bliss, ecstasy; riches.
   R wealth corrupts; unhappiness.

Necromancy

The meaning of necromancy is divination
through communication with the dead.
Despite the popular conception (created and
maintained over the years by scores of horror movies)
that it involves bringing the dead back to life,
using black magic and producing zombies, necromancy
is no more than a form of brief mental contact
between our world and the spirit world.

PLANCHETTES AND OUIJA BOARDS

Generally, the communication with the dead that produces divinatory messages uses a planchette or a ouija board. There is some similarity between these two and they are often confused with each other.

A planchette is a mobile writing device. It is a small board supported on free-running castors an inch or so above the surface on which it moves – usually a table. Attached is a pencil that just touches a large piece of blank paper laid on the table. Several people simultaneously each rest a finger very lightly on the planchette, neither trying to push it nor obstruct it. With luck, the planchette may move across the paper leaving written words in its wake.

Of course, to obtain any useful response from the planchette the conditions must be suitable. The room should be dimly lit, perhaps by candles to create the right atmosphere. The participants need to be genuinely interested in receiving a message from the spirit world, and at least one of them should be sensitive to spirits so that he or she can be used by the spirit to move the planchette. On occasion the planchette can give astonishing results, with the spirits of the dead providing details of the future, but not often.

ABOVE *A group using a planchette on a ouija board to spell out messages.*

ORIGINS OF THE OUIJA BOARD AND MAKING YOUR OWN

While the planchette is claimed to have been known to the ancient Chinese (who greatly revered the spirits of the dead and frequently communicated with them), the ouija board is of much more recent origin. It dates only from the last few years of the nineteenth century and was thought up by an American, William Field. He may have had hopes of contacting foreign-speaking spirits, since he named his invention after the French and German words for 'yes'.

The planchette and, in particular, the ouija board, have been popular as games, sometimes for young people and even for children. This is unfortunate, as neither device is intended to be a game. Any communication with the spirit world is a serious matter which, if undertaken carelessly, may be frightening or lead to considerable emotional trauma, and may be psychically dangerous.

A ouija board is generally made of wood, polished and shiny. It has the letters of the alphabet, the numbers 1 to 9, and a few useful words such as 'Yes', 'No', 'Repeat', 'Hello' and 'Goodbye' painted on it. These may be either in a circle around the board or arranged in

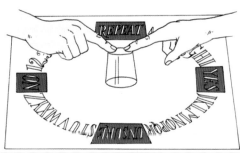

ABOVE *A ouija board being used with a glass.*

rows or arcs, somewhat resembling a typewriter keyboard. The moving part may be a planchette on castors, with some kind of pointer. As when using a planchette to write, the fingers of the participants should touch the planchette only lightly. An alternative is to make your own ouija board, utilizing any polished wood surface, with the letters, numbers and words written on separate cards and using a drinking glass upside down to slide from letter to letter.

Questions are asked aloud and the answers are spelled out by the movement of the glass.

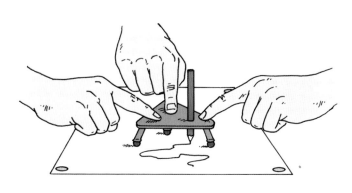

ABOVE *A planchette being used for spirit writing.*

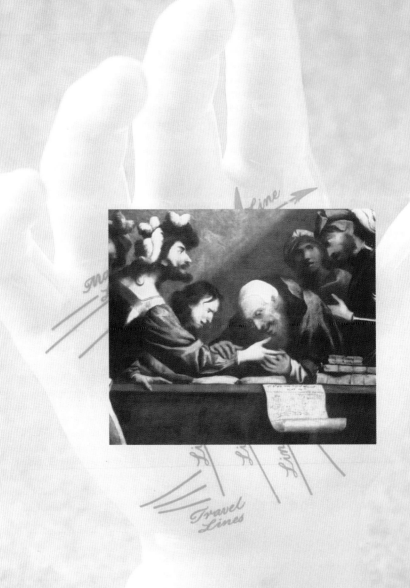

Palmistry

Divination by means of examining the hands
(not just the palms, despite the popular name) is of great
antiquity. A better name is cheiromancy, from the Greek
word *cheir*, meaning hand. It is supposed to have originated
in China over 5,000 years ago and to have spread from
culture to culture across Asia and the Middle East to
Greece, where Aristotle wrote on the subject in about 340
B.C. The Romans brought it from Greece to Western
Europe and it was developed gradually over the centuries
by scientists such as Paracelsus (a Swiss physician of the
sixteenth century) and Cheiro (Count Louis Hamon,
the greatest of the nineteenth-century palmists). The claim
that it was started by the Gypsies, or even brought to
Europe by them, has no basis in fact.
Today, palmistry is still very popular in the West, perhaps
because it seems so simple, requiring no equipment. Yet it is
deceptively complex, demanding much knowledge and
experience if it is to be practised with any accuracy.

Anyone who does practice cheiromancy in a proper manner will not attempt to give a reading without careful consideration of both the subject's hands. The left hand shows the subject's potential from birth while the right hand reveals present character and future events. If the subject is left-handed it is the other way around. The lines always vary between a pair of hands. They are present from the moment when a baby is born, and they change slightly during the course of the years.

HANDSHAPE

- A *practical* hand, with a broad palm and short fingers, indicating a down-to-earth, hard-working, industrious nature.
- An *intuitive* hand, with a long palm and short fingers, indicating a quick, restless person, tending to be an individualist.
- A *sensitive* hand, with a long palm and long fingers, suggesting a person of strong emotions and imagination, and perhaps a volatile or introverted character.
- An *intellectual hand*, with a short palm and long fingers, suggesting an orderly, clear-thinking person, perhaps articulate.

An older classification system recognizes seven hand shapes. It is even claimed that different hand types mean a suitability for different careers.

In addition, the general texture of the skin on the hands is important – coarser or finer reflecting a 'coarser' or 'finer' personality – together with the consistency of the hands, ranging from hard through firm, rubbery and soft, to flabby.

Several shapes of fingers are recognized, each revealing a particular type of individual. The set of the fingers in relation to the hand (whether one begins lower on the palm than others), the closeness of the fingers, and the relative lengths of the different fingers and joints all have their various meanings.

FINGERNAILS (ONYCHOMANCY)

The fingernails, too, are classified, with the following meanings.

- *Short, broad nails:* critical, quick-tempered, lacking in self-control.
- *Short nails:* enthusiastic, scientific.
- *Long, broad nails:* rational, perhaps with good judgement, timid.
- *Long, oval nails:* easy-going, serene, courteous.
- *Wedge-shaped nails:* very sensitive.
- *Large, squarish nails:* sad, cold, perhaps selfish.

It is worth remembering that, however, well-manicured or neglected – or even chewed – the fingernails are, they will reveal their basic shapes and their owner's characteristics.

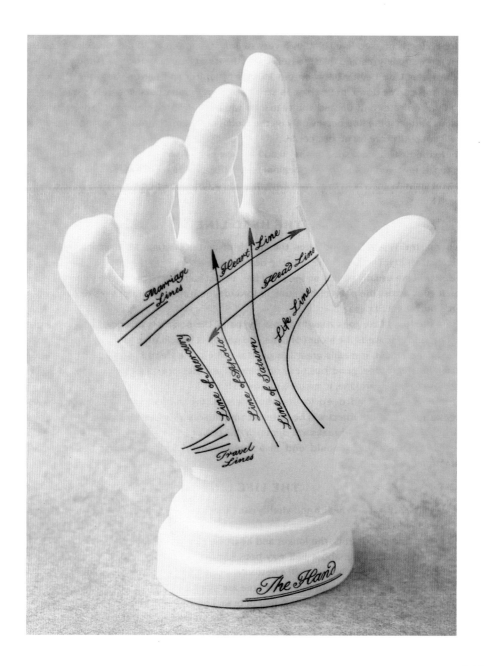

Reading fingernails is a whole, complex area of divination in itself, known as onychomancy (from *onyx*, the Greek word for a nail).

THE THUMB

The thumb, of course, has a similarly wide range of shapes. A long thumb suggests powers of leadership, while a very long thumb might be the sign of a tyrannical person. A large thumb denotes a capable, strong-minded, energetic type, and a small thumb suggests one lacking willpower and energy. A flexible thumb denotes tolerance and extravagance, while a stiff one indicates reserve, caution, even stubbornness. The thumb's thickness, positioning and the nature and relative lengths of the joints have additional meanings, especially when these factors are taken in combination with all the other features of the hand.

THE PALM

Both detailed diagrams of the palm and your own hands usually display a bewildering variety of lines and areas. On diagrams these are all carefully named, but on your own hand they are often difficult to identify, or even to find at all. Do not be put off by this. Concentrate on finding the three clearest lines first. They are the Heart Line, the Head Line and the Life Line.

THE HEART LINE

The Heart Line is the line controlling temperament and emotional health. Its shape and strength are generally taken as signs of the person's capacity for love.

The normal starting point for the Heart Line is on or just below the Mount of Jupiter, at the base of the index finger. From here it may drop down a little before running straight across the hand. A long, clearly marked line signifies a very steadfast, warm-hearted person. Where the Heart Line is more strongly marked than the Head Line, the Heart Line rules the head (and vice-versa).

If the Heart Line begins between the Mounts of Jupiter and Saturn (between the first two fingers) and curves down, the person is said to be very sympathetic and very sensual. A faint Heart Line indicates only limited ability to love, while a Heart Line closer to the fingers suggests a jealous nature. If the line begins only on the Mount of Saturn, the person may still be sensual, but will not really care for other people.

Where the Heart Line begins on the Head Line, the person will be the envious kind. If the Life Line, too, is involved in a three-way beginning, the disposition is probably unreasonable.

Lots of small branches to the Heart Line indicate a flirtatious person. Breaks in the line or a chained line suggest unfaithfulness.

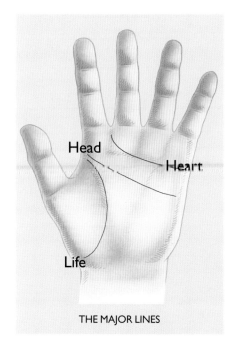

Head

Heart

Life

THE MAJOR LINES

it reaches the mount, it means great imagination. Where the Head Line slopes the other way, towards the Heart Line, good business or financial abilities are suggested, although if it runs along close to the Heart Line, it means a narrow outlook.

If the line is clear and deep for its whole length, the subject will have great powers of concentration, and the subject will be able to commit himself or herself unswervingly to a task. However, any 'chaining' or breaks will diminish this power.

Ideally, the Head Line should end in a three-pronged fork, indicating strengths in business ability, imagination and intelligence.

THE HEAD LINE

In general, the Head Line indicates the depth of understanding, level of intelligence and intellectual ability. The longer the line, the better.

The Head Line usually begins on the Life Line, almost halfway between the thumb and index finger. It goes across the palm either straight towards the Upper Mount of Mars or curving down towards the Mount of Luna.

Where the Head Line goes straight across the palm, the person is practical, a good organizer. If the line slopes towards the Mount of Luna, the person is imaginative with a sensitive nature. If

THE LIFE LINE

Not only longevity but also health and vitality can be foretold from this, probably the best known of all lines on the palm.

The longer and clearer it is, the longer and healthier your life will be. Normally the Life Line starts from the Head Line, about halfway between the thumb and index finger, indicating a controlled personality. If it begins with a netted effect it suggests a cautious person.

Branches from the Life Line to the Head Line are significant. A forked beginning suggest an ability to understand and help others. A pair of branches up to the Head Line from close to the beginning denotes an inheritance or a good start in life. A branch halfway down indicates success in middle age. Where the Life Line reaches right to the wrist, life will be long, probably until well over 70 years of age.

A tasselled or shallow line suggests lack of vitality, though not necessarily a short life. Breaks in the line are indicative of changes in lifestyle or problems with health.

THE MOUNTS

Before you try to identify the other lines, which are all less clearly marked, it will help you to learn the names of the various areas of the palm. These are known as mounts, despite the fact that in many people they are hardly any higher than the areas around them and in some cases they are even hollows.

The great importance of the mounts is that whichever of them is most highly developed on your hands gives its qualities most strongly to your personality and to your health.

If you bend your hand right back at the wrist and hold it up at eye level you will be able to see more easily which

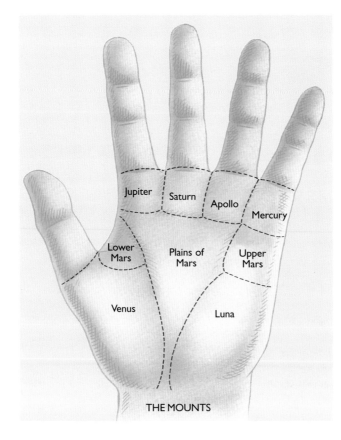

Jupiter
Saturn
Apollo
Mercury
Lower Mars
Plains of Mars
Upper Mars
Venus
Luna

THE MOUNTS

of your mounts is most highly developed. Often two or three mounts are equally developed, giving a well-balanced character that is made up of the qualities of both or all three. Occasionally, all the mounts seem to be about equal, in which case the personality will be equable and life will most likely be smooth and happy.

Because all the mounts have their good and bad aspects, the markings on the most prominent mount or mounts must be studied carefully. The general rule is that vertical lines are good signs and horizontal lines are bad signs, although a hatching of vertical and horizontal lines to form a grille is a bad sign, while a star is a good sign.

Here are some of the main characteristics of people who have a particular one of the mounts predominating:

The Mount of Jupiter An ambitious honourable person, perhaps a leader; likely to marry young, liable to digestive problems resulting from a love of good food; a cross on the mount indicates a happy marriage.

The Mount of Saturn A tall, thin, gloomy person, relatively unsociable; a good student, and possibly very musical; perhaps will remain unmarried; may suffer from illnesses such as rheumatism and nervous complaints.

The Mount of Apollo Happy, healthy, athletic and very appreciative of art; will marry, but not happily; may suffer from heart trouble.

The Mount of Mercury Most easily led into illegalities, especially if the mount shows a grille; otherwise, good in business and at games; generally healthy except for a tendency to suffer minor stomach problems.

The Mount of Mars A complex type because of the upper and lower sections of the mount and the Plain of Mars between. This person will be a fighter, mainly aggressive if the lower section predominates and resistive if the upper does; if the plain is well developed, the subject will be short-tempered; this is a stubborn, persistent individual, healthy and energetic.

The Mount of Luna An expressive person of great imagination, but a dreamer, tending towards the impractical; of weak health.

The Mount of Venus A loving, considerate and generous individual, happy though not good in business (as tends to be too honest); may be passionate and often tempted by attraction to the opposite sex; tends to marry young and to be very healthy.

THE MINOR LINES

THE LINE OF FATE

Of the minor lines on the palm, the most important is the Line of Fate (or Line of Saturn), which is normally (but by no means always) present for part of the way between the wrist and the Mount of Saturn. It is the career line, indicating how successful and how settled you are and will be in your chosen career. If it begins on the Mount of Luna this suggests success in your profession – but with considerable help from a member of the opposite sex. If it begins in the middle of the palm and

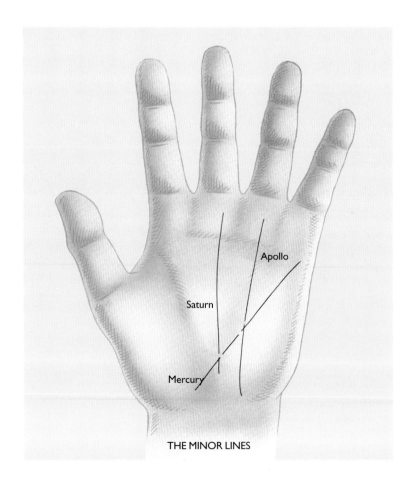

THE MINOR LINES

runs all the way to the Mount of Saturn it indicates success through your own efforts. Where the line begins further up the hand, this means an uneventful, perhaps idle or unsuccessful early life.

A sharply defined Line of Fate is most propitious. Where it is thin it means you need to work very hard for success; where it is chained it suggests difficulties. If the line is absent altogether (or only very shallow) you may still be able to overcome this handicap and achieve some success. A bar cutting across the Line of Fate denotes a serious obstacle, and a break in the line means a complete change. If the line continues after a break, look carefully to see whether it does so a little closer to the thumb (indicating an improvement in your general career situation) or away from it (the opposite).

Sometimes the Line of Fate does not end on the Mount of Saturn but runs across (perhaps via a branch) to the Mount of Jupiter, indicating a great success through ambition, or to the Mount of Apollo, indicating some artistic success. If the line ends short of the Mount of Saturn it may mean an early end to your career or merely an eventful later career.

THE LINE OF APOLLO

The Line of Apollo (or Success) is not found on all hands. Where it does exist

it ends on or close to the Mount of Apollo, although its beginning may be on the Mount of Luna, the Plain of Mars or the Life Line. It is, generally, a sign of the prospect of accomplishment, and the longer the line the more will be accomplished. As with the Line of Fate, it can be age-linked, with its presence closer to the Mount of Apollo indicating success in later life. Also, if the line is absent, wavy or chained, you can expect little success, and breaks or bars indicate there will be set-backs or barriers to success.

THE LINE OF MERCURY

The Line of Mercury (or Health) runs towards the Mount of Mercury, sometimes from the wrist end of the Mount of Luna. While a clear, deep line suggests a life free from illness so, ironically, does an absence of the line. A chained line predicts liver troubles, a broad, shallow line indicates stomach problems, while dots, bars and breaks on the line suggest illness to come at those age points. An island on the line is the worst of all signs, indicating suffering to come.

Many other minor lines exist, at least on some people's palms, so, if you have a real interest, you should consult a book on the subject.

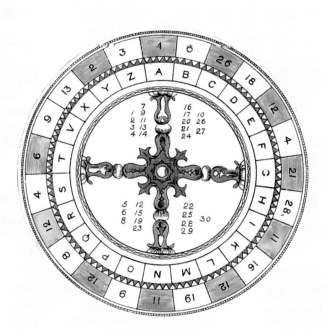

Numerology

Numbers control all our lives. It is very simple
to calculate which particular number or numbers
represent you and then to look up the prophecies
associated with those numbers. Numerology
(or anthromancy, as it is sometimes known) is easily
mastered, requiring no great amount of knowledge,
no apparatus and no skill. It is an ancient form
of divination, but it has connections with
astrology and, as with the tarot, its origins
have been lost in the mists of time.

Numerology

The only complexity (or uncertainty) about numerology is that there are many slightly different systems to which this chapter is only a brief introduction. In most cases you need to calculate a single-digit number that represents you. Most important is your birth number, because this should reflect your innate characteristics. Also of significance, because it reflects your development through life, is your name number.

FINDING YOUR BIRTH NUMBER

To find your birth number, first add up the day, month and year figures of your date of birth.

For example, if your date of birth is **June 15, 1966**, you need to add **6** (June is the sixth month) **+ 1+5** (the days as separate figures) **+ 1 + 9 + 6 + 6** (the year) which gives **34**. To arrive at a single number, simply add the two digits **3 + 4, giving 7**.

This is the birth number.

An alternative approach, equally simple, was suggested by Cheiro, the famous late-nineteenth-century palmist and numerologist.

Here the year and month are ignored, so that the birth number is determined by your day of birth alone. A person born on the first day of the month has the birth number of 1. But so also does the person born on the 10th, 19th or 28th (add the digits

together, ignoring zeros). Under this system, the person born on June 15th 1966 has a birth number of 6 (+5) as does anybody born on the 15th of any month of any year.

FINDING YOUR NAME NUMBER

If you want to find your name number, write down the most commonly used form of your name (not necessarily your full name) and convert the letters using the table below.

But once again there is another approach. An older system of number-letter equivalents (supposedly of very great antiquity) leaves out the number 9. This is because the number 9 represents the 9-letter name of God and must not be used. It is an old Hebrew taboo. (In the Jewish faith, even the spelling out of the name of God is taboo and is often written rather as 'G-d'.

1	2	3	4	5	6	7	8	9
A	B	C	D	E	F	G	H	I
J	K	L	M	N	O	P	Q	R
S	T	U	V	W	X	Y	Z	

C H R I S   M O R G A N

| | | | | | | | | | |

3 + 8 + 9 + 9 + 1 = 30   4 + 6 + 9 + 7 + 1 + 5 = 32

3 + 0 = 3   3 + 2 = 5   And 3 + 5 = 8

So this name number is 8.

1	2	3	4	5	6	7	8
A	B	C	D	E	U	O	F
I	K	G	M	H	V	Z	P
Q	R	L	T	N	W		
J		S		X			
Y							

Using this system provides a different name number
as shown below.

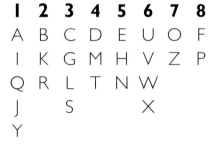

C H R I S   M O R G A N

| | | | | | | | | | |

3 + 5 + 2 + 1 + 3 = 14   4 + 7 + 2 + 3 + 1 + 5 = 22

1 + 4 = 5   2 + 2 = 4   And 5 + 4 = 9

So this name number is 9.

MEANINGS OF NUMBERS

1 One represents the beginning, the One (in the sense of a creator) and also the Sun. People with this number have great leadership qualities, sometimes with enough success, dominance and aggression to be ruthless. So it is a powerful number. Use your power carefully and others will look up to you. Use it carelessly and you may be guilty of being self-centred and tyrannical. This number equates with the tarot card The Magician. Your best days (of any month) are the 1st, 10th, 19th and 28th, especially when one of them falls on a Sunday (although Monday is almost as lucky for you). Your best colours are brown and yellow and your lucky stones are topaz and amber.

2 The Moon is associated with number two. It is a 'feminine' number, gentle and intuitive, more concerned with thought than action. Compatibility is great with One people. Twos are inventive and articulate. Beware of indecisiveness, a lack of self-confidence and deceit. Your best days are the 2nd, 11th, 20th or 29th and any Monday. Your colours are green, cream and white and your stones are Jade, pearl and moonstone. Your tarot card is The High Priestess.

3 Three is a creative number, its people tending to be disciplined and successful. Jupiter is the guiding planet. The best days of the month are the 3rd, 12th, 21st or 30th, with Thursdays particularly good. Your relationships will be especially fruitful with other Threes. Beware of a tendency towards bossiness. Your colours are in the mauve, violet and purple range. Your stone is amethyst. Your tarot card is The Empress.

4 Because four is a square and thus a complete number, representing the seasons, people born under its influence may be square (in the sense of dull), earthbound and unimaginative. These people seem to delight in being rebellious, taking an opposite view to everyone else. Making friends is difficult so, if this applies to you, you must beware of feeling too lonely and isolated. Your lucky days are the 4th, 13th, 22nd and 31st, you are represented by the planet Uranus, and Sunday is your best day. Bright blue and grey are your colours and sapphire is your stone. Your tarot card is The Emperor.

5 Symbolized by Mercury, Five is the number of the senses. Its people are mercurial – impulsive, unpredictable, active, eloquent and ever-changing. Sensual pleasure is important here (from the five senses). Number Five people have the knack of making friends easily with anybody (especially with other Fives). Your greatest flaws are being highly strung and hating routine or restrictions. Your lucky days are the 5th, 14th and 22nd and Wednesdays. Most lighter colours suit you and your stone is diamond. Your tarot card is The Hierophant.

6 The emotions are important with Six because of the influence of Venus. The love represented is more romantic or family love than sexual It is a 'perfect' number because it is the sum of its factors (1, 2 and 3). Number Six people tend to be reliable, domestic and fond of beauty. If you are a Six you know that you can also be obstinate. But even so, you will be very popular, making many friends. You have many lucky days: the 3rd, 6th. 9th, 12th, 15th, 18th, 21st, 27th and 30th, as well as any Friday. You can wear any shade of blue or pink. Your lucky stones are turquoise and emerald and your tarot card is The Lovers.

7 Most significant of all the numbers, Seven is generally thought of as lucky because there have been so many famous groups of seven or of its multiples: the days of the week, phases of the Moon, notes of the musical scale, colours of the spectrum, the seven original fixed stars, the seven graces, the seven virtues and, from the Bible, seven days of creation, seven trumpets, seven plagues, seven seas and many more. Its great mysticism is summed up in the belief that a seventh son of a seventh son will possess enormous magical powers. So the number is regarded as highly spiritual and philosophical. Its people are intuitive, perhaps psychic, and not interested in material wealth. If you are a seven person, you have great associations with water, your planet being Neptune, so you will tend to love travel, especially on the sea. You often have power over others, but must avoid being too introverted. Your originality can make you a good writer, poet or painter. The 7th, 16th and 25th are your lucky days, together with any Monday. Your best colour is green and your stone is moss-agate. The associated tarot card is The Chariot.

8 Eight is a strange and contradictory number in which there are echoes of the rebelliousness of Four. Governed by Saturn, number Eight people must suffer sorrow along with any success. If you are an Eight person, you possess great willpower and individuality, yet you are always misunderstood, partly as a result of hiding your strong feelings beneath a cold exterior. You must try to be more open, less intense, and strive to make friends. Your best days are Saturdays and the 8th. 17th and 26th days of the month. Dark colours suit you best, in the range of dark grey, black, dark blue and purple. Your stone is amethyst, a dark sapphire or even a black pearl. Your tarot card is Strength, and strength is what you need to triumph over such an unlucky number as Eight.

9 A number as sacred as Seven, Nine is numerologically the ultimate because when multiplied by any other number it reproduces itself ($3 \times 9 = 27$, then $2 + 7 = 9$). It has Biblical connections (a trinity of a trinities and the nine orders of angels, for example), represents the nine months of pregnancy, the nine spheres of ancient cosmology and the nine lives of a cat. Nines are active, determined, fighters (the influence of their planet Mars), accident-prone, quarrelsome and impulsive. They get on well with Threes and Sixes. If you are Nine, your lucky days are the 3rd, 6th, 9th, 12th, 15th, 18th, 21st, 24th, 27th and 30th, and Tuesdays. Your colours are ruby, garnet and bloodstone. Your tarot card is The Hermit.

NUMBERS OVER NINE

What the numerologists call 'secondary numbers', those over 9, are also sometimes used in determining fortunes. Up to 52 (the weeks in a year) they all possess meanings, and up to 22 they have strong connections with the tarot pack's Major Arcana,. For example, 11, 12 and 13 (Justice, The Hanged Man and Death, respectively)

are held to be unlucky numbers, while 17 (The Star), 19 (The Sun) and 21 (The World) are fortunate, boding well for future events.

Why should numbers over 9 be significant at all, when they can all be reduced so easily to single digits? The answer is that sometimes these secondary numbers are obviously important in a person's life, with the same number recurring. For example, suppose that you were born on the 12th day of the month (or, especially, on the 12th of December), that you are constantly ranked 12th in exams, that you marry on the 12th, live at house number 12, divorce after 12 years and so on it would seem folly to ignore such a number and abbreviate it (1 + 2) to 3. Such a number, influential or fateful, is known as a 'fadic' number (perhaps from *fado*, the Portuguese word for fate).

ABOVE *A numerological 'wheel of fortune', originating from the seventeenth century.*

NUMBER THIRTEEN

The number 13 is almost always considered unlucky. In America in particular, some buildings do not have a floor numbered 13, and some hotels have no room 13. In Italian theatres there are often no seats numbered 13.

This belief that 13 is an unlucky number may originate from the tarot pack, where number 13 of the Major Arcana is Death. Alternatively, there may be a connection with Judas Iscariot, the thirteenth man at the Last Supper. Although 13 is the traditional number of witches in a coven, whether it has been deliberately chosen by witches to parody the Last Supper is unclear. A 'Baker's

dozen' of 13 loaves is supposed by one theory to mean the Devil's dozen, from *Boucca* (an old English name for a spirit).

In fact, there seems to be no truth in the idea of 'unlucky 13'. For some people it is a fadic number of great good fortune. Certainly it has never been unlucky in Far Eastern cultures, and the formation of the original 13 states of the American Union has not proved unlucky. A good example of the number 13 being lucky was James Buchanan (13 letters), a Pennsylvanian (13 letters), who was the 13th president of the United States.

Crystallomancy

Crystallomancy, or divination by looking into
a crystal ball, is the only variation of scrying
commonly used today. Scrying (simply an old English
word for seeing) was practised by
many early civilizations.

Crystallomancy

Originally, a clear, still pool of water was used for the purpose, and one can still look into a bowl, bucket of water, a mirror or a pool of ink for predictive shapes, although this is not much done these days. This form of divination is known as catoptromancy. Even a polished surface of metal or stone may be used for scrying. The important point about all these methods is that there must be a reflective surface upon which the scryer can fix his or her attention.

CRYSTAL BALLS

LEFT *Crystal balls are usually made of glass and spherical.*

Crystal balls have increased in popularity in the West in recent years. Rock Crystal was originally used. Beryl is better for the purpose, and even more expensive. Most crystal balls today are made of clear glass; even so, they can cost a great deal of money.

It is far better (for psychic reasons) to be given a crystal rather than to purchase one yourself. If you must buy one, it is best to avoid mail order. It is essential that you always handle the crystal before purchasing it to make sure that it feels right to you. A size of about 10 cm/4 inches in diameter is best, but the size and shape must suit you personally. Most crystals sold today are spherical in shape, though some have a flat side ground into them so that they can be free-standing without a support; there are others which are oval. The shape is a matter of personal preference.

PREPARING YOUR CRYSTAL

Once you have your crystal, you must prepare it for use. Different scryers offer different advice for this, although most recommend a careful wash. Running water is best, especially from a natural source such as a stream. Rainwater collected and poured over it will probably suffice. Then rinse the crystal with vinegar and polish it with velvet or chamois leather. The crystal must always be kept clean and out of bright or direct light. Keep it carefully wrapped in a piece of black velvet or black silk when you are not using it.

Some say that the crystal needs to be charged up with psychic energy, either just when it is new or each time before use. This charging may be done simply by the scryer holding the crystal in his or her hands and consciously willing it to be energized by the spirit world.

SETTING THE SCENE

There is little agreement among scryers as to the best conditions for crystallomancy. Quietness is preferred, although some scryers are willing and able to operate in the bustle of a psychic fair, surrounded by other fortune-tellers and their clients. Dim light is also preferred, so that there are no reflections to interfere with images seen in the crystal, but a few scryers can function well in bright conditions, and a few prefer complete darkness. Twilight is usually regarded as the most propitious time for scrying.

Whether or not your subject (questioner) should be given the crystal to handle before the scrying is a matter of sharply divided opinion; there are some scryers who always give the crystal to their subject, whereas others feel that it would ruin a crystal if anybody else touched it (the subject may, however, be asked to put his or her hands close to it). In any case, the subject should be present and be thinking about a problem

or question. The scryer must be in a tranquil and receptive state of mind. For a few minutes the scryer will see nothing, and then images will begin to appear in the crystal.

WHAT THE 'CLOUDS' SAY

For most scryers the crystal becomes misty first, and as the mist clears, the true visions of the future can be seen. These are often no more than cloudy masses. Here the colour is important.

White is the best, signifying good luck. Green clouds mean there is hope. Blue clouds, too, are a good sign. Yellow means jealousy. Red and orange clouds are signs of danger, perhaps of hatred. Worst of all is black, which portends evil.

When a question is being asked by the subject, the clouds can supply an answer by their direction, with rising clouds meaning 'yes' and descending clouds meaning 'no'.

Some scryers can distinguish shapes and even scenes from the future. The shapes are most often symbolic, with fairly obvious meanings – a skull suggesting death and so on. It is further claimed that the position of the shape or picture in the crystal can indicate time, with future events right at the front and past events at the back.

If you are trying to tell fortunes from a crystal and are seeing nothing, do not despair. It takes a good deal of practice and concentration. You must persevere.

Cartomancy

Cartomancy is the word for telling fortunes
with ordinary playing cards. It is a form of divination
that has been around for almost as long as the cards
themselves, from the early Middle Ages.

Cartomancy

Over the years many different predictive meanings have been given to the individual cards and to the combination in which they appear. Some card readers recognize changed meanings for reversed cards (as in tarot readings) while others do not. A further complication is that most readers seem to employ their own, quite various methods as to the number of cards used and the manner and order of laying them out. Consequently, this chapter can give only some indications of a very diverse and varying method of fortune telling.

THE PACK AND THE SUITS

The standard British and American pack of playing cards consists of 52 cards arranged into four suits. The suits are hearts, clubs, diamonds and spades. Each suit contains the numbered cards one (Ace) to ten and the court cards: a Jack, a Queen and a King. This is different from the tarot pack and different also from the packs in common use in continental Europe.

PSYCHIC ELEMENTS

Later on, this chapter will explain some methods of laying out the cards and something about interpreting them for fortunes. But you must not think of this as a mechanical procedure that anyone can perform. In order to read the future in cards, you

need to be sensitive to the overall meaning of the cards that turn up and at the same time, be sensitive to the person whose fortune you are trying to read. There are psychic elements to cartomancy in the way that there are to many other methods of divination.

GENERAL TIPS

You can improve your chances of giving an accurate reading in several ways. One is to buy a new pack of cards and reserve them for fortunes. If you wish to consider the more negative meanings of reversed cards, you will need to do something such as mark one end of the pack with a pencil. Do not let other people handle your cards except for the questioner at the start of a reading (who should be allowed to cut them, at least). Make sure that the conditions suit you – the correct light level and no distractions. Take your time shuffling the cards. Never rush through a reading. Use a prompt sheet of interpretations if you need to, but let your inner feelings guide you. You are advised not to read your own fortunes in the cards, nor indeed to perform a reading for somebody who is not present.

You can either deal cards from the whole 52-card pack for your reading or else you can reduce it to a 32-card pack. This is done by discarding the twos, threes, fours, fives and sixes of each suit. The 32-card is more commonly used by professional card readers.

COMPARING CARD PACKS

Type of pack	Number of cards	Suits	Court (or Face) cards
UK & US	52	Hearts, Clubs, Diamonds, Spades	Jack, Queen, King,
Tarot	78	Cups, Staves,/Batons, Coins/Pentacles, Swords	Page, Knight, Queen King
French	52	Hearts, Trefoils, Tiles, Spades/Pikeheads	Valet, Queen, King
German	36	Shields, Leaves/Flowers, Hawk bells, Acorns	Unter, Ober, König
Spanish	52	Cups, Staves, Coins, Swords	Jack, Queen/Knight King
Italian	40	Cups, Staves, Coins, Swords	Page, Knight, King

THE CARD MEANINGS

Particular combinations are ignored here, and the meanings are given for the 32-card pack only. **R** means the card is reversed.

HEARTS

ACE romantic love, friendship, a happy home life.
R unsettled at home.
KING a good-natured, fair-haired man, offering sound professional advice.
R an unreliable person.
QUEEN a fair-haired woman, faithful and affectionate.
R spiteful person.
JACK a friend, a happy young person.
R short-tempered.
TEN an excellent card; ambitions achieved; by, love, luck.
R short-term problems.
NINE wishes fulfiled; good health; improvements all round.
R temporary setbacks.
EIGHT invitations, visits, pleasurable journeys, perhaps romance.
R unrequited love.
SEVEN wisdom, imagination, self-sufficiency.
R boredom.

CLUBS

ACE happiness, wealth and good health.
R short-lived happiness.
KING a dark-haired man, honest and generous.
R small troubles.
QUEEN a dark-haired woman, romantic and capable.
R initiative, craftiness.
JACK a reliable friend, skilful and enterprising.
R an insincere lover.
TEN unexpected money coming.
R trip, minor problems.
NINE immediate achievement, sudden opportunity.
R disappointing receipts.
EIGHT a gamble; choose your partner carefully,
R unhappy in love.
SEVEN small benefits; goodwill from repayments.
R small money problems.

DIAMONDS

ACE a letter or a ring; important.
R bad news.
KING an obstinate man, powerful, fair-haired.
R deception penetrated.
QUEEN a flirtatious fair-haired woman.
R a spiteful gossip.
JACK an official (perhaps a relative); unreliable.
R troublemaker.
TEN changes involving money, a trip, jobs.
R similar, but with problems.
NINE surprise; beware of self-interest.
R domestic disputes.
EIGHT pleasant trips; a late marriage.
R beware of hasty romance.
SEVEN social chat; news.
R tiny problems magnified.

SPADES

ACE love affairs, perhaps unhappy; caution needed.
R bad news, bad luck, death.
KING an ambitious dark-haired man, a bad enemy.
R an unscrupulous enemy.
QUEEN a dark-haired widow, unscrupulous.
R a crafty and spiteful person.
JACK a rough diamond, well-meaning.
R an untrustworthy person.
TEN worry, unhappiness, emotional distress.
R illness, loss.
NINE all-round bad luck; conflict and loss.
R unhappiness, misfortunes.
EIGHT trouble approaching; illness and anxiety.
R sorrow in relationships.
SEVEN worries, perhaps imagined.
R bad advice, indecision.

SPREADING THE CARDS

Note that the details of particular spreads are not fixed by any laws; different readers use slight variations.

As with the significator in tarot readings, a client card may be selected to represent the client or questioner; if it is a fair- or red-haired younger man or woman use the King or Queen of Hearts respectively. For a fair- or grey- or red-haired older man or woman it should be the King or Queen of Diamonds. If a darker-haired younger man or woman, the King or Queen of Clubs. For a darker-haired older person, use the King or Queen of Spades.

BELOW *Spanish (top row), German (centre row) and Italian (bottom row) playing cards.*

A SIMPLE CARD-READING SYSTEM

If you lack expertise in card-reading, try this simple system first. Shuffle a 32-card pack carefully, especially end-to-end, to produce plenty of reversed cards. Then remove the top and bottom cards and lay them aside, face down, as a surprise for later.

Cut the 30 cards and deal them face down into three equal piles. Turn up the top pile and spread them into an overlapping row so each card is visible. Look for any reversed cards and push them a little way down, out of line, for easier recognition. This row represents the questioner's past.

Now do the same with the middle and bottom rows, which represent the questioner's present and future respectively. The three rows may be read (taking note of reverses). Finally, retrieve the two surprise cards and turn them over. They may add a different slant to the whole reading.

THE FAN

After shuffling the 32-card pack, lay it face down on the table, well spread out. Then invite the questioner to choose 18 cards. Lay these out face up in the order shown, (see picture). It is important that the client card or significator should be among the first 13 laid out. If not, the seven of the same suit will do. If neither is present,

THE SIMPLE SYSTEM

try another spread, or abandon the reading until another time.

Look at cards 1 to 13. Find the client card and, counting that as the first of a group of five cards (moving to the right), give a reading of the fifth card. This card then becomes the first of a new group of five as you move to the right again. Continue to interpret the fifth card each time until, eventually, your fifth card is the client card (which you must also interpret). Then move to the five cards laid out beneath the others. Interpret the end one (cards 14 and 18) together, then cards 15 and 17 together, and finally card 16. This should provide a fairly good general forecast of the questioner's life.

THE GRAND STAR

This is a more detailed spread of 21 cards, popular, useful and of long standing. It may also be done from the full 52-card pack, when it is known as the Wheel of Fortune (as shown).

Place the significator face up in the middle of the table and then lay out the first 21 cards of the shuffled pack face down in the order shown. Now begin the reading, interpreting cards in pairs. In addition to their specific meanings, the cards above the significator should be taken as representing the questioner's future accomplishments, while those below it refer to past successes; to the left are potential obstacles, and to the right is a source of help.

The 21 cards must be turned over and read in this order: 13 and 15, 20 and 18, 19 and 17, 9 and 5, 11 and 8, 10 and 6, 12 and 7, 3 and 1, 4 and 2, then card 21 on its own.

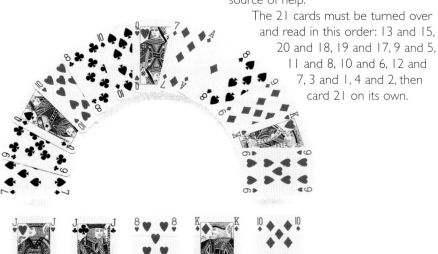

THE FAN

THE GRAND STAR

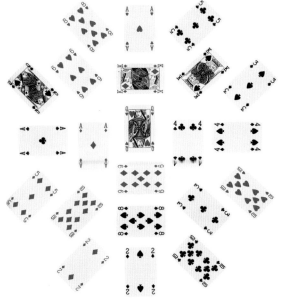

DO WALSH'S SYSTEM

Here is an example of a personal method of divination practised by a card-reader known to the author. It is simple and may or may not be unique to her. A 32-card pack is used. The questioner or client asks a question (aloud or silently) while shuffling the cards and cutting three times. The reader deals the top 12 cards into three equal piles. It is the centre pile which is the most important, and is turned over and interpreted first. Either the top card is turned over and read on its own, or else the four cards in the pile are turned and read together, depending on the reader's instinct.

If necessary the left-hand pile is interpreted next, then the right-hand pile. In this system, combinations of cards are regarded as being very significant.

Clearly, much more must be put into this reading than just the standard meanings of the cards, which is the way it should always be with divination from playing cards.

THE DO WALSH'S SYSTEM

Dreams

We all dream, every night, although most of the time we do not remember doing so. Some of these dreams are predictions of future events. Even if we can recall our dreams, it is difficult to decide which ones are predictive and even more difficult to cut through the mass of symbolism to determine their true meanings successfully.

Dreams

'Dreams are true while they last, and do we not live in dreams?'
Alfred. Lord Tennyson.
'Learn from your dreams what you lack'. *W. H. Auden.*
'I had a sort of dream-trance the other day, in which I saw my favourite
trees step out and promenade up, down and around, very curious – with
a whisper from one, leaning down as he pass'd me. We do all this on the
present occasion, exceptionally, just for you'. *Walt Whitman.*
'Existence would be intolerable if we were never to dream'. *Anatole France.*

RIGHT *An 1843
woodcut of a
scene from the
Bible, in which
Joseph interprets a
dream of the
Pharaoh.*

DIFFERENT
KINDS OF SLEEP

Research has shown that there are two
different kinds of sleep. One is identified
by twitches of muscles in the face and
body, by slightly irregular breathing, by an
increase in blood pressure and by
movements of the eyeballs beneath the
eyelids. Because of this last characteristic
it is known as REM or rapid-eye-
movement sleep. The other type of sleep
is quieter, with few body movements,
regular breathing and no rapid eye
movements. It is called NREM or non-
rapid-eye-
movement sleep.
Every night we
alternate
between these
two types of
sleep,
experiencing
about 90 minutes
of each, though
REM-sleep periods become slightly
longer and NREM-period shorter
towards morning. If people are
awakened from REM sleep they nearly
always report that they were dreaming; if
awakened from NREM sleep they hardly
ever do.

So we know that REM sleep is
associated with dreams and that people
generally dream for about half their
sleeping time. Furthermore, it has even
been suggested that dreaming is a more
vital activity than sleep itself. Perhaps we
sleep only in order to dream.

DREAMS AND DIVINATION THROUGH THE AGES

Dreaming has always been regarded as a strange, mystical activity. Using the odd, half-remembered scenes of happenings of our dreams to help predict the future is a very ancient form of divination which is known and used all over the world. It is called Oneiromancy, from *oneiros*, the Greek word for a dream.

Some of the earliest written records in existence, from Mesopotamia and ancient Egypt, are concerned with dreams and their interpretation. There was a strong and widely held belief in the ancient world that dreams foretold the future.

The Bible describes many dreams that contained detailed instructions or symbolic messages. The most famous is Jacob's dream of a ladder set up between Earth and Heaven.

Genesis 28: 12–16;. Ancient Greek and Roman literature is full of references to dreams. One early work on the subject has survived, Oneirocritica by Artemidorous of Daldi, a Greek, who flourished in about 140 A.D. He believed that the main function of dreams was to enable us to discover the truth by way of symbolic images.

'Dreams and visions are infused into men for their advantage and instruction', he wrote. His book is a collection of dream interpretations, which remained the major work on its subject until the nineteenth century.

BELOW *Cats are generally omens of good luck to a dreamer.*

SOME HISTORICAL PREDICTIVE DREAMS

There have been many important predictive dreams recorded over the centuries, which have influenced the lives of the great. Julius Caesar was persuaded by a vivid dream to cross over the Rubicon (a small river) into Italy in 49 B.C., setting off civil war. It is reported that Napoleon Bonaparte used messages from his own dreams in the planning of his military victories. James Watt, one of the inventors of the steam engine, developed ball bearings thanks to a persistent series of recurring dreams. Abraham Lincoln was warned of his assassination in a dream, but chose to ignore it. Adolf Hitler, claimed that, when only a corporal in a front-line trench by the Somme during World War I, he was warned by a dream to get up and leave the bunker where he was sleeping. He did so, and very shortly afterwards the bunker was completely destroyed by an incoming shell.

DREAM INTERPRETATION TECHNIQUES

If we are to stand any chance of arriving at an accurate interpretation of our dreams, there are certain techniques to be learned in the recording, classification and de-symbolizing of our dreams.

1 While the details of a dream are usually extremely vivid and detailed as we experience them, with colour, sound and sometimes other sensory information, such details fade away rapidly upon waking. By the time we have got up and had breakfast only dim outlines may remain. So it is essential to keep paper and pencil beside your bed and to write down all details as soon as you wake.

2 Many dreams are clearly not foretelling the future. It could be that a simple external cause is responsible. If the bed is too warm you may dream

ABOVE *Powerful and frightening images may appear in a nightmare.*

of ovens or of sweltering under the hot desert sun. Likewise, an external noise might be integrated into your dream without being intrusive enough to wake you up. Indispositions, such as a headache or indigestion, may give rise to a particular dream, as may a television programme you have just viewed or an unusual occurrence during the day. All such simple associations, once noted, may be easily identified and the dreams eliminated as not being of the predictive kind.

3 Two other categories can also usually be ignored. Dreams early in the night are said not to be predictive, and dreams full of the details of everyday existence will probably have no predictive significance. Even so, such dreams should be noted at once, for practice and for easier elimination.

Of the dreams remaining, in those containing unusual and probably predictive elements, certain motifs recur. In fact, there are a few motifs that recur in almost everybody's dreams and which have widely accepted interpretations.

Here are a few examples.

Flying This is an image of imminent success, a sign of rising above mundane annoyances, indicating your desire to be in charge of events. But if your flying dream ends in falling, this is a bad sign, suggesting insecurity, fears of failing and the strong possibility of falling out with someone you know well.

Hotels This is a bad sign because of the impersonality and uniformity of hotels. Dreaming of a hotel suggests that you have a fear of being swallowed up by an organization with a consequent loss of personal identity.

Weddings The old belief that dreaming of a wedding is a literal prediction of a wedding in the family has largely been largely superseded by the new, symbolic meaning of an alliance to come, most likely in the business sense, although it could also spell romance.

Nakedness While this used to be accepted as a prediction of exposure of our darkest secrets, it is today thought of more as a fear of our vulnerability being exposed.

Lakes or water Images of water represent our emotions. Interpreting the exact message is difficult and depends partly on the state of the water in the dream. Murky water is a symbol of ill fortune. Clear, sparkling water can indicate a spiritual rebirth. Generally, water means unseen complications ahead, and it may represent the depths of and dangers from other people.

I Ching

The I Ching is a system of wisdom and prediction
that is claimed to be well over 5,000 years old.
It is a Chinese system that was not introduced to
the West until the twentieth century, where it has come
to enjoy general popularity only in the last
couple of decades or so.

Yin, Yang and the Trigrams

The bases of the *I Ching*, which may be translated as 'The Book of Changes', are the unbroken line and the broken line, and the change from one to the other.

The unbroken line is called Yang. It signifies the answer 'yes', the positive, the active, the projective and traditionally, the 'masculine'.

————

The broken line is called Yin. It signifies the answer 'no', the negative, the passive, the receptive and traditionally, 'feminine'.

—— ——

From these two lines, eight three-line variations are possible. These are

known as the trigrams. Their invention is credited to Fu Hsi, the legendary first Emperor of China, who lived around 2,000 B.C.

HEXAGRAMS

These trigrams can be paired up in 64 combinations to produce the *I Ching* itself, which consists of 64 hexagrams. Each hexagram has a very complex meaning that can be interpreted as a view of the future, or as an answer to

TRIGRAMS

Sign	Name	Associated Image	Attributes	Family Link
☰	Ch'ien	Heaven/Sky.	Strong/powerful	Father
☷	K'un	Earth	Faithful/submissive	Mother
☳	Chen	Thunder	Impulsive/provocative	Eldest son
☵	K'an	Water/The Deep	Dangerous/flexible	Middle son
☶	Ken	Mountain	Unmoving/inevitable	Youngest son
☴	Sun	Wind/Wood/Air	Subtle/penetrating	Eldest daughter
☲	Li	Fire/Sun	Enlightening/warm	Middle daughter
☱	Tui	Marsh/Mist/Lake	Joy/magic	Youngest daughter

It should be realized that there is much more complex symbolism to each of the trigrams than this.

a question or problem. The philosophical wisdom of the *I Ching* is a mixture of Taoism and Confucianism. The oracle of judgement of each hexagram is ancient and poetic. The commentary or interpretation of this is traditional and is very detailed, dealing in turn with the questioner's material prosperity and business relationships, love and friendship.

In order to get to the correct hexagram for your own question or problem or situation, you need to use a random-choice system. The systems used generate one line at a time so must be repeated six times to provide a hexagram.

There are two complications which need to be explained first. One is that the first line produced goes at the bottom of the hexagram, and each successive line is written above the previous one. The second complication is that there are not just Yang — and

Yin – – lines but Yang becoming Yin ─⊙─ and Yin becoming Yang ─✕─ . These last two are 'moving lines' and a complete book of the *I Ching* will give readings for them in each line of each hexagram. Also, once the lines have moved (changed) the hexagram will be different, and that hexagram should be consulted too.

USE OF YARROW STALKS OR COINS

The random-choice system can be operated either with 49 yarrow stalks or with three coins. Using yarrow stalks is more complex, and may take half an hour or more, so here we will stay with coins, which are no less traditional. The Chinese use special coins, which are circular and usually have square central holes, but any coins will do. Heads are given a value of 3 and tails 2.

During the tossing of the coins, the person wishing for an answer must keep his or her question in mind meditating on it. The three coins are tossed together onto a flat surface and the score is noted. The only possible scores are 6, 7, 8 or 9. While 7 means a normal Yang line — and 8 a normal Yin line – – 6 gives a moving Yin ─⊙─ and 9 a moving Yang ─✕─ . If you toss the coins six times, write

LEFT *Producing hexagrams by using yarrow stalks is a complex process.*

A HEXAGRAM EXAMPLE

$7 =$ —— ——

$7 =$ —— ——

$7 =$ —— ——

$6 =$ —✳— —✳—

$8 =$ — — — —

(first number) $6 =$ —✳— —✳—

down the score each time (working upwards), then convert each of the numbers to a line, you will end up with your hexagram, such as that below.

This is hexagram 12, which has two moving lines. After the change it will be hexagram 13, to the right.

The extra symbolism of the moving lines will not be given here, but the interpretations of hexagrams 12 and 13 can be looked up and compared in the table following:

TABLE OF MODERN I CHING

1	2	3	4	5	6	7	8
9	10	11	12	13	14	15	16
17	18	19	20	21	22	23	24
25	26	27	28	29	30	31	32
33	34	35	36	37	38	39	40
41	42	43	44	45	46	47	48
49	50	51	52	53	54	55	56
57	58	59	60	61	62	63	64

SOME SIMPLIFIED INTERPRETATIONS
OF THE 64 HEXAGRAMS

1 YANG Follow the plan calmly. Do not rush. Work hard. Do not try to overreach yourself.

2 YIN Wait. Allow others to lead, for your happiness is in their hands. Co-operate with them.

3 GROWING PAINS Advance very slowly and carefully. Be content with this, but ask others for guidance.

4 YOUTHFUL IGNORANCE Find a teacher and learn to use your strength. Follow good advice. Be humble and persevere.

5 WAITING Beware of danger. Wait and build your strength. The path will become clear. Friends will help you.

6 CONFLICT Conflict approaches, yet it is futile. Sway with the wind; accept criticism. Wait for improvement.

7 SOLDIERS Be ready for battle. Be organized and disciplined. You may or not need to fight. Others will help you.

8 SEEKING UNION Work with others and peace and harmony will come. Be diligent and persevering.

9 MINOR RESTRAINT Be restrained and sensible. Plan for hard times. Success will come later.

10 TREADING Keep to the straight path. Walk it courageously, without hesitation or evil intent.

11 PEACE Great gifts will come if you share your happiness. Peace comes from the powerful and weak uniting.

12 DISJUNCTION Keep your head down during a period of stagnation, and growth will come.

13 SOCIETY Work with others and you will emerge from obscurity. There is light for you at the end of the tunnel.

14 WEALTH Work and study. Don't try to impress others. Don't be conceited. Support the cause of good against evil.

15 MODESTY Humility brings power and success. Others will help if your attitude is right.

16 ENTHUSIASM Inspire helpers with your own enthusiasm. Avoid arrogance and self-satisfaction.

17 FOLLOWING Drift with the stream. Let others lead. Your time of success will come.

18 FIXING Discover a problem and rectify it. Apologize if necessary. Be honest and energetic.

19 CONDUCT Having achieved authority, be generous and cautious. Changes are coming.

20 CONTEMPLATION Look carefully at the world around you. Be penetrative. Do not wait.

21 BITING THROUGH Stress your virtues and achievements, however small. Ignore the jealousies of other people.

22 BEAUTY Attractive, showy appearances are worthwhile only if they bring results. Afterwards remember to be frugal.

23 COLLAPSE Beware of weakness and collapse. Prepare to rebuild. Guard against inside treachery.

24 RETURNING Timing is vital. The cycle changes. Renew your energies. Watch and be patient.

25 THE SIMPLE Be honest, simple unselfish. Do not rush in. Recognize your limitations.

26 MAJOR RESTRAINT You have strength and power. Show restraint. Work hard. Be ready when your time for success comes.

27 NOURISHMENT Wait and remain watchful. Practise moderation in speech and consumption. Persevere.

28 GREATNESS IN EXCESS Know your own strength and weakness. Great changes are imminent.

29 THE DEEP Beware of danger. Be consistent and true to yourself. Wait for the path to be revealed to you.

30 FIRE Be intellectual and logical. Beware of burning out. Accept some dependence.

31 TENSION Avoid all envy and excessive ambition. Be yourself. Perseverance will bring you success.

32 CONTINUITY Avoid haste. Be casual. Occupy your space, but focus on a goal.

33 RETREAT Watch out for traps and people trying to take advantage.

34 GREAT STRENGTH Do not bluster. If you use strong words be prepared to act on them. Keep to your path.

35 ADVANCE Effortless progress, but make sure that you are open and honest. Good fortune awaits you.

36 DARKENING OF THE LIGHT In times of depression and gloom be cautious and flexible. Do not complain. Better times approach.

37 THE FAMILY Deal with any problems now. Concentrate on your surroundings and family.

38 NEUTRALITY Be flexible in small things. Reconcile any differences.

39 DIFFICULTY Adapt to difficult circumstances. Remove or sidestep problems. Request and offer help.

40 RELEASE Settle an acute situation quickly. Do not let yourself be held back. Advance with confidence.

41 DECREASE Share your wealth freely with those who deserve it most.

42 INCREASE Seize your opportunities. Accept luck but do not expect it to last.

43 BREAKTHROUGH Watch for dangers. Ensure against them. Stay firm and thwart evil.

44 TEMPTATION Do not be influenced by the strong. Use calm persuasion to influence other people. Caution.

45 ACCORD If you face opposition, either go with the crowd or recruit an ally.

46 PUSHING UPWARDS Great things can only be created by slow, steady growth. Keep moving upwards to your goal.

47 REPRESSION Look into yourself to cope with a problem. Have confidence. Stay calm and continue to persevere.

48 THE WELL Monotonous work must be done. Be generous. Watch out for tricks.

49 REVOLUTION Watch the changing of events. Choose your moment. You will appear better to other people.

50 THE CAULDRON Check all details. Accept small losses but work to eliminate large ones.

6I THE THUNDERCLAP Great movement or stormy weather. Be composed and make plans.

52 KEEPING STILL Rest and build up strength. Do not rush, gamble or take on too much. Look inwards.

53 PROCESSION Push forwards slowly. Almost imperceptible progress is better than stagnation.

BELOW *The legendary Emperor Fu Hsi is said to have invented the trigrams.*

54 THE MARRYING MAIDEN Be content with what you can get. More opportunities will come.

55 ABUNDANCE Be inwardly happy and even in worse times you will achieve success.

56 THE STRANGER You may need to travel or project yourself. Inner strength and outer modesty are both needed.

57 THE PENETRATION OF THE WIND Gentleness and reasonableness are required. Obtain advice. Bend with the wind.

58 PLEASURE Your strong spiritual feelings will be reflected by others. Serenity brings riches.

59 DISPERSION Take important decisions now. Do not be inflexible or swept away. Success will come.

60 RESTRAINT Be cautious and moderate. Do what you can in a difficult situation. Follow the rules.

6I UNDERSTANDING Listen for warnings. Be cheerful and gentle. Endure what you must.

62 SMALLNESS IN EXCESS Even the weak can achieve much. Avoid over-ambition. be cautious and content in yourself.

63 COMPLETION Consolidate your success. Look forwards, but remain alert to the present.

64 ALMOST THERE Advance with caution. Judge carefully and take your chance when it comes.

Other Methods of Fortune Telling

There are a few other ways in which fortunes can be told,
although they are not thought of as 'proper' fortune telling.
Some of the these mentioned in this section include
Tasseomancy – name for reading patterns in tea leaves,
Pyromancy – judging the future from the way a flame burns,
Dowsing – using a stick, traditionally used to find water,
Phrenology – feeling the shape of the skull,
Dominoes and Dice.

Other Methods of Fortune Telling

TASSEOMANCY

Tasseomancy is a fancy name for divination from the patterns of tea leaves at the bottom of a cup. It has the virtue of being a cheap and simple method of fortune telling, with no special equipment or skills required. Probably it has been in use in the West since the seventeenth century, soon after tea became popular among Europeans. In China the practice of tasseomancy is believed to have been in existence since ancient times.

There are a few simple rules. You should use a plain white teacup (not a mug), preferably broad and shallow. Any pattern or extra shape (fluting, for example) makes a reading more difficult. Do not use very fine, dusty tea, or the shape will be confusing; a large-leafed tea is best.

For the fortune to concern you, you must drink from the cup, leaving just a little liquid at the bottom, enough to cover the leaves. Then, holding the cup in your left hand, swirl the liquid gently three times in an anti-clockwise direction while thinking of a particular problem or question. Invert the cup over a saucer and leave it for a few seconds so that all the liquid drains off. When you turn the cup the right way up again, the reading can begin.

Study the leaves carefully, from different angles, for any recognizable shapes. Sometimes it is better to half-close your eyes, so that indistinct shapes achieve a little more regularity. It may be that there is nothing there, and forcing yourself to imagine a shape is

BELOW *Reading the tea leaves in the bottom of a cup is an old tradition.*

no good at all. Or it may be that with careful scrutiny you can make out some object—a full moon, perhaps, or an arrow, or a ball and chain.

The shapes are usually symbolic and fairly easily understood. For example, a full moon retells a love affair; an arrow suggests imminent bad news and a ball and chain denotes unpleasant obligations. Note that all of the shapes must be read together as part of the whole fortune, not in isolation from each other.

But it is not only the shape of the leaves that is important; their position in the cup must also be noted. Because you naturally hold the cup by its handle, the handle represents you, the inquirer. Generally, the closer any shape in the leaves is to the handle, the more it will affect you (or perhaps your

family). If it points away from the handle it is receding from you, and if pointing towards the handle it is approaching you. Shapes near the rim of the cup are in the present or near future, while those at the bottom or the side are still far in the future. The bottom of the cup is an unlucky area.

BELOW *Map for reading the tea leaves; the inquirer holds the handle of the cup.*

LOCATION OF EVENTS

USING COFFEE GROUNDS

If you are a person who does not drink tea, or who uses only tea bags, coffee grounds may be interpreted in exactly the same manner, providing you drink ground coffee, unstrained. The meanings of shapes are mostly the same as for tea, but because of the fineness of the grounds there are a few differences. For example, a triangle denotes luck coming your way, while wavy lines refer to a trip, a square means joy, and a cross foretells suffering and death in the future.

USING MOLTEN LEAD OR WAX

An older variation of tasseomancy which is still occasionally practised is to melt a little lead or wax and drop it into cold water. The resulting shapes may be interpreted as tea leaves. With lead this is properly known as molybdomancy and with wax as ceromancy.

In parts of continental Europe it is the custom, on New Year's Eve, to use molybdomancy in order to discover what the coming year will bring. Others hope to see the initial letter of the name of the person who they will marry formed in wax. Obviously it is safer to handle molten wax (candle wax will do) than molten lead.

PYROMANCY

Some of the oldest forms of divination in the world involve burning.

Pyromancy is an umbrella term for the various methods. It can refer to several things: judging the future from the way different substances burn (the brightness or steadiness of the flame and the presence or absence of sound); using the amount, colour and behaviour of smoke as an indicator; throwing an odd number of straws onto a red hot surface and watching the way in which they move as they shrivel and blacken; placing marked stones in a fire as a Halloween custom and inspecting their condition the next morning, with an undamaged stone being a good omen for the coming year; writing a wish on a piece of paper and tossing it into a fire in a grate so that it either burns (your wish will not come true) or it is carried up the chimney by hot air (your wish will come true); looking for predictive pictures in a fire.

The last three of these are still practised today. The method for the last is to begin with a coal fire that has been burning for a while and has reduced itself to glowing, half-consumed coals. Toss a small handful of salt over the fire, then sit down in front of the fire and, once the salt has burned off, scrutinize the embers. It is best done on one's own, in peace and quiet, preferably at night with no lights on. What you are looking for is any recognizable shape among the flaming coals.

Some of the luckiest shapes to be seen are a cat, a clover leaf, a mountain or a pair of shoes. Any kind of tree or pillar signifies an approaching love affair. An eagle, any type of flower, a hatchet or sword are unlucky omens.

DOWSING

Traditionally, a dowser sought hidden water or mineral deposits with a divining rod, which was most often a forked twig of hazel (although a thin, pliable twig of willow, birch, apple or beech could be used just as well). These days, the dowser is more likely to have a pair of rods – plain, L-shaped

BELOW *Searching for water can be helped by the use of dowsing.*

wires with the shorter axis of each held loosely, and the longer axes, parallel to each other, pointing out to the front. Such rods are easily made from wire coat hangers.

The system is that the dowser walks forwards holding the rods out in front of him or her, and thinking of the objective. When that objective, water, (or perhaps a metal pipe) is beneath the dowser, the rods move to signify that fact. A hazel twig normally jerks up (sometimes down) quite sharply, while a pair of rods either cross or move apart. Dowsing is, of course, a form of prediction, because the dowser is predicting that a certain thing will be found at that point.

Many people possess the power to dowse in this way, and dowsing has often been used by public utility companies to locate buried water pipes or cables.

DOWSING FOR ANSWERS

Less well known is the fact that dowsing can be used to give a 'yes' or 'no' answer to a wide range of questions.

The first stage (usually a matter of trial and error) is to discover, for a particular person using a particular type of rod, which reaction of the rod or rods signifies 'yes' and which signifies 'no'. Then any question may be asked, so long as there is a clear 'yes' or 'no' answer. For example, if the depth of the pipe or water source is needed, specific questions must be asked about different depths. For example – 'Is the water less than ten feet down?' or 'Is the water between ten and fifteen feet down?' and so on.

Extending this just a little, it is possible to get a person to lie down beneath the rods and to discover all sorts of information about them. For instance, 'Is this person aged less than 30 years?', 'Does this person have a IQ of more than 100?', 'will this person still be alive in ten years's time?'. Sometimes the rods fail to react, but with expertise and patience, a detailed set of predictions may be built up.

The rods – any rods – are crude and awkward compared with a pendulum. The traditional use of a pendulum for divination was as a method of predicting the sex of an unborn child. The mother-to-be would suspend her wedding ring above her stomach by a hair from her head. If the pendulum swung in a circle the baby would be born a girl and if it swung back and forth it would be a boy. This form of divination (with a wedding ring) is known as dactylomancy.

The pendulum, however, is much more versatile than this. As with dowsing rods, its 'yes' and 'no' reactions

need to be calibrated. Then there are no limits. Because of its small size it may be used with pinpoint accuracy. For example, it can be held over a map to predict where a pipe, a cable, a water source or even a dead body will be found. It can be asked the location of any lost object. It can be used to predict anything about the future. The only proviso is that the question must be framed so as to produce a definite 'yes' or 'no' answer.

Try these techniques for yourself. They are cheap, simple and may give astonishingly accurate predictions.

SORTILEGE

Sortilege means divination by the casting of lots. Early forms of dice and marked pebbles existed in most ancient cultures; they were used for divination as well as for games.

THROWING DICE

With such varied origins, it is not surprising that many different systems exist today for throwing dice and interpreting the future from the results. Here is perhaps the simplest and most widespread system, briefly described.

Draw a circle about 30 cm across. Take three

standard dice (i.e. each being six-sided and spotted 1 to 6), shake them in your hand or in a cup, and throw them into the circle. A dice ending up outside the circle may well foretell upset plans, while two outside denotes a quarrel and all three outside suggests that you do not know the strength of your wrist!

The three dice, in the circle, show upper spots adding to a number from three to eighteen. Each of these totals has a meaning.

3	luck, a surprise
4	unpleasantness
5	a wish coming true
6	loss
7	business problems or scandal
8	external influences
9	love and marriage
10	birth
11	parting or illness
12	good news
13	grief
14	help from a friend
15	care needed
16	travel
17	changing plans
18	great success

USING THE CIRCLE

A refinement of this is to divide the circle into 12 equal segments, standing for different areas of your life. Moving clockwise from 12 (as on a clock) the areas are: enemies, friends, your work, your state of mind, legal things, love and marriage, health, the present, domestic items, travel, finances, next year. Each dice landing in an area may now be interpreted individually.

SCORES

1	basically good
2	success depends on others
3	great success
4	problems
5	good indications
6	uncertainty

DOMINOES

Turning to dominoes, the method is to lay the set of 28 face down on a flat surface and mix them. Then draw three dominoes and turn them up.

DOUBLE-SIX – money gained, success

SIX-FIVE – membership in an organization

SIX-FOUR – wrangles leading to a loss

SIX-THREE – a trip, improvement

SIX-TWO – a gift is coming

SIX-ONE – a solution soon to your problem

SIX-BLANK – beware of false friends

DOUBLE-FIVE – a successful house move

FIVE-FOUR – take care of a good investment

FIVE-THREE – a visit from a benefactor

FIVE-TWO – a birth

FIVE-ONE – a love affair,
perhaps unhappy

FIVE-BLANK – help a friend in
need

DOUBLE-FOUR – you will
attend a stranger's party

FOUR-THREE – push aside
your unfounded worries

FOUR TWO   beware of a
false friend

FOUR-ONE – a temporary
financial setback

FOUR-BLANK – repair a torn
friendship

DOUBLE-THREE –
problems from a
rival in love

THREE-ONE – a
revelation will help

THREE-TWO –
beware of bad luck for
a few days

THREE-BLANK –
jealousy will mar a
friendship

DOUBLE-TWO – you will
help a happy marriage

TWO-ONE – beware of
losing a personal
item

TWO-BLANK –
happiness from a new
encounter

DOUBLE-ONE – move
boldly now and you will win

ONE-BLANK – help from a
stranger

DOUBLE-BLANK – the worst omen:
loss and unhappiness

PHRENOLOGY

Phrenology was invented in the eighteenth century by the German Dr. Franz Joseph Gall. He considered that the shape of the skull reflected the shape of the brain and thus was an indication of character. Various areas of the head correspond to aspects of character, and the relative sizes of the phrenological parts of the head reflect particular aspects of personality. These aspects include such things as cautiousness, spirituality, mirthfulness and hopefulness. Phrenology was extremely popular during the first part of the nineteenth century; it has only a relatively small following today.

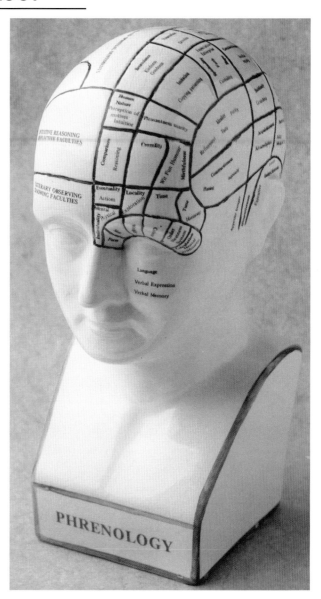

RIGHT *Heads marked with the regions of the skull are used by phrenologists.*

Superstitions

Superstitions may be ignorant and irrational beliefs in the supernatural (to paraphrase a dictionary definition) but we still take note of them. Even hardheaded rationalists who scoff at such things will, most likely, perform some sort of superstitious ritual every day. They may note early morning precipitation and mutter, 'Rain before seven, fine before eleven'. At a moment of crisis they may cross their fingers for good luck. If they find a four-leaf clover they will be pleased, and would think twice before walking under a ladder or opening an umbrella indoors.

Superstions and Omens

Nearly all superstitions are omens, that is, signs of a particular future event, either good or bad. Of course, some of these future events are neither good nor bad in themselves – they may refer to weather, to the arrival of a visitor or to the identity of a husband-to-be.

Some of our superstitions are very ancient. Many can be accounted for; to take an example, if we spill salt and toss some over our left shoulder it is because the devil is supposed to stand there, so the salt will go into his eye. A few, particularly weather predictions and medicinal remedies, have been validated by science. For example, foxglove tea was treatment for heart disease centuries before medical research showed that foxgloves contain digitalis, which is a powerful heart stimulant.

Not all superstitions are old by any means. Some have sprung up in recent years, noticeably those concerned with motor vehicles. For instance, it is regarded as unlucky to buy a car painted green or a car in which somebody has died.

ABOVE *One cup is broken: two more cups will break subsequently.*

A WORD OF WARNING

Generally, the power of good-luck omens is lessened or perhaps nullified if you seek them deliberately. And a lucky or unlucky appearance (such as that of an animal) is worth bothering with only if the creature in question is uncommon in the area. For example, do not expect good luck (in Britain) or bad luck (in the United States) every time a black cat crosses your path if the cat is your own pet.

SOME SUPERSTITIONS IN THE HOME

● if you drop a spoon, a visitor is to be expected.
● if you drop a fork, the visitor will be female.
● If you drop a knife, you will receive a male visitor.

● If two women pour coffee or tea from the same pot, one of the two will be pregnant before the end of the year.

BAD LUCK OMENS

● Forgetting to put the lid on a coffee-pot or teapot before pouring means that a stranger is coming with bad news.

● If you break a cup you can expect to break two more the same day (breakages are supposed to go in threes – like many other bad luck and good luck occurrences). The only remedy is to break the heads off two matches.

● Leaving Christmas decorations up in the home after the Twelfth Night.

● Putting your left shoe on before your right.

● Taking eggs into or out of the house during the hours of darkness.

● Bringing lilac, May blossom or a sprig of broom into the house.

● A bat flying into the house.

● Having peacock feathers around the house (this is very unlucky).

● Breaking a mirror in the house gives seven years' bad luck. This is based on the belief that the human body renews itself every seven years and therefore it will take that long for all of the bad luck to disappear.

RIGHT If one horseshoe brings luck, what must many bring to the household?

PRECAUTIONS TO TAKE IN THE HOME FOR GOOD LUCK

● Nail a horseshoe to the door of your house (so long as the ends point upwards).

● Sneeze three times before breakfast.

● Spill your drink when you propose a toast.

● Spill a box of matches.

SOME SUPERSTITIONS IN THE STREET

LUCKY OMENS

● Meeting the same person by chance twice while you are out on business (which is a particularly lucky omen).

● A strange dog following you home.

● Picking up a pencil in the street.

UNLUCKY OMENS

● Meeting a grave-digger.

● Dropping your umbrella.

GLOSSARY

aeromancy divination from the air and sky, particularly concentrating on cloud shapes, comets and other phenomena not visible in the heavens.

air signs these are the signs of Gemini, Libra and Aquarius.

angles these are the Ascendant (ASC), Descendant (DSC), Midheaven (MC), and Innum Coeli (IC), referring to the cusps of the first, seventh, tenth and fourth houses, respectively.

arithmancy the earlier form of numerology where divination is made through numbers and the number value of letters.

ascendant the degree of the zodiac rising over the eastern horizon of the birthplace at the moment of birth. This degree forms the first house cusp of a horoscope and is of great personal significance in the character and life of the individual.

astraglomancy a form of divination by dice where the faces of the dice bear numbers and letters.

astrology divination using celestial bodies: the sun, moon, planets and stars.

augury the general term for the art of divination and is chiefly applied to interpretations of signs and omens.

aura a subtle quality or atmosphere emanating from a living being, object or place.

austromancy divination by the study of the winds.

bestial signs Aries, Taurus, Leo and Capricorn – so named because they are symbolized traditionally as animals.

bibliomancy divination by books.

bicorporeal signs Gemini, Sagittarius and Pisces. Also called double-bodied and double signs, they are associated with twins and dual experiences.

cardinal signs these are the signs of Aries, Cancer, Libra and Capricorn, and are related to the change of the seasons.

cartomancy is fortune telling using cards such as the Tarot.

catoptromancy is an early form of crystal gazing that utilizes a mirror turned to the moon to catch moonbeams.

chart a horoscope.

chiromancy is divination from the lines of people's hands.

clairvoyance is 'clear seeing' of divinatory information. Parapsychologist generally regarded as a form of extrasensory perception.

common signs Gemini, Virgo, Sagittarius and Pisces, synonymous with mutable signs.

constellation from the Latin 'constellation' set with stars. A group of fixed stars.

critical degrees classic critical degrees are 0, 13 and 26 degrees of cardinal signs

(Aries, Cancer, Libra and Capricorn); 8-9 and 21-22 degrees of fixed signs (Taurus, Leo, Scorpio and Aquarius); and 4 and 17 degrees of mutable signs (Gemini, Virgo, Sagittarius and Pisces).

cusp the beginning of a house in the chart. Also, a cusp of a sign is the degree when one sign ends and the other begins.

cycle A planet's zodiacal period; the time it takes a planet to make a complete revolution of a horoscope.

descendant the cusp of the seventh house of the astrology chart. This point is directly opposite the ascendant.

diurnal signs Libra, Scorpio, Sagittarius, Capricorn, Aquarius and Pisces – signs whose natural positions are in the diurnal or southern hemisphere of a horoscope.

double signs, doubled-bodied signs synonymous with bicorporeal signs – Gemini, Sagittarius and Pisces. See bicorporeal signs.

dowsing or **divining rods** are methods of divination where a forked stick is used to locate water or precious minerals.

earth signs these are the signs of Taurus, Virgo and Capricorn.

electional astrology a branch of astrology in which favourable times are elected, or chosen, in advance.

elements the signs are

divided into four elements: Fire, Earth, Air and Water.

ephemeris an almanac that lists the zodiacal positions of the planets and other astronomical data.

equal house horoscope One in which twelve equal houses are derived by taking successive arcs of 300 each, beginning with the Ascendant and completing the zodiac circle.

event chart a horoscope drawn up according to the date, time and location of a particular happening, interpreted to gain insight into influences surrounding the event and an outlook for possible developments stemming from that event.

fire signs these are the signs of Aries, Leo and Sagittarius.

fixed signs these are the signs of Taurus, Leo, Scorpio and Aquarius.

fruitful signs the water signs – Cancer, Scorpio and Pisces, which are associated with fertility.

grand trine this aspect pattern involves three points (three or more planets may be involved) that form mutual trines to each other. When lines are drawn from each planet to the other in a natal chart, a triangle results.

glyphs these are the symbols used for the astrological signs, planets and luminaries and aspects.

hard aspects are generally considered the conjunction, opposition and square. In midpoint work, the hard aspects also include the semi-square and

sesquiduadrate.

horoscopy is the practice of casting of astrological horoscopes.

houses the horoscope divides the heavens into 12 houses. each house has rulership over specific areas of life.

luminaries the Sun and the Moon.

masculine signs these are the signs of Aries, Gemini, Leo, Libra, Sagittarius and Aquarius. The remaining six signs of the zodiac are feminine signs. Masculine signs are also referred to as 'positive' signs.

metoposcopy is the reading of character using the lines of the forehead.

midheaven this is the sign and degree of that sign on the cusp of the tenth house of the natal chart. It is the highest point in the zodiac at the moment of birth, and in relationship to the place of birth. abbreviation: MC

mutable signs these are the signs of Gemini, Virgo, Sagittarius and Pisces.

natal chart horoscope drawn for a person's birth.

oneiromancy is the interpretation of dreams and their prophetic nature.

orb when determining whether one planet forms an aspect to another, astrologers allow an 'orb' of influence, which is a specific number of degrees.

palmistry is the broad field of divination and interpretation of the lines and structure of the hand.

part of fortune an Arabic part, and likely the most

common one. Wherever the part of fortune is found in the natal chart is the place where they are thought to have a natural affinity.

personal planets these inner planets and luminaries include Sun, Moon, Mercury, Venus and Mars. They have a personal and direct effect on the native's personality.

phrenology is the long practiced study of head formations.

planetary rulers each sign is ruled by a planet.

quadrants there are four 'quadrants' in a chart, and each starts at the cusp of the first, fourth, seventh and tenth houses.

retrograde a planet is considered 'retrograde' when it appears to be moving backwards.

soft aspects are generally considered the sextile and trine aspects.

synastry the art of relationship astrology.

tasseomancy is the reading of tea leaves that remain in the tea cup once the beverage has been drunk.

tarot cards a set of (usually 72) cards that include 22 cards representing virtues and vices and death and fortune etc.; used by fortune-tellers.

water signs these are the signs of Cancer, Scorpio, and Pisces.

zodiac is a circle of 360 degrees, divided into 12 equal sectors of 30 degrees each that are the astrology signs.

INDEX

A

Air signs, 50
Alfred, Lord Tennyson, 194
Almagest or *Tetrabiblos* (Four
    Books),16
Anthromancy *see*
    Numerology, 171
Aphrodite, 17
Apollo
    the Mount of, 167
    the Line of, 169
Aquarius, 31, 50, 51, 53,
    124–130, *125–6, 128, 130*
Aries, 31, 50, 53, 54–60,
    55–6, 58, 60
Astrology 6–8, *6*
    brief history, 14–19
    Chinese, 35
    electional
    history of, 13
    Mesopotamian, 15
    Western, 21–33
Auden, W. H., 194
Aztecs, 15

B

Babylonia, 6, 13
    Nabu, 15
Babylonian
    astrology, 18
    boundary stone, *14*
Babylonians, 14, 15, 17, 22
Baker's dozen, 177
Bedosus, a Chaldean priest,
    17
Birth number, 172
birth of Jesus, The, *19*

Boar, the, 35
Bonaparte, Napoleon, 196
Boucca, 177
Buffalo, the, 35, 37

C

Cancer, 31, 50–2, 75–81,
    76–7, 79, 81
Capricorn, 31, 50, 53,
    117–123, *118–19, 121,
    123*
Card meanings, the, 186–7
Cardinal sign of Aries, *51*
Cartomancy, 183–191
Cassiopeia, 19
Cat, the, 35, 39
Caesar, Julius, 196
Celestial Art of Astrology, The,
    24
Celtic spread, the, 149, *150*
Chaldeans, 19
Chariot, the, 143, *175*
Cheiro (Count Louis
    Hamon), 161, 172
Chinese astrology, 35
Chinese zodiacal vase, *15*
Clubs, 185–6
Crystallomancy, 179–181,
    180
Cockerel, the, 35
Count Louis Hamon, *see*
    Cheiro
Cups, 153

D

Dali, Salvador, 140
Diamonds, 187

Death, 145, 176–177
Dee, John, 24
Devil, the, 146
Dog, the, 35, 46
Dominoes, 213
Do Walsh's System, 191, *191*
Dowsing, 207, 211, *211*
Dinner party fortune telling,
    8–9
Dragon, the, 35, 40
Dreams, 193–7, *194, 195,
    196*

E

Earth signs, 50
Electional astrology, 33
Emperor, the, 142, 174
Empress, the, 142, 174
Enunia Anu tablets, 15

F

Fan, the, 189, *190*
Fate, the line of, 168
Fingernails (Onychomancy),
    162
Fire signs, 50
Flying, 197
Fool, the, 141
Fortune telling
    dinner party, 8–9
Four Books *see*
    Almagest or *Tetrabiblos,* 16
France, Anatole, 194

G

Gemini, 31, 50–2, 68–74,
    69–70, 72, 74

Gnosticism, 19
Goat, the, 35, 43
goddess Nut, *17*
Grand Star, the, 190, *191*
Great Bear, 18
Great Fire of London, 24, *24*
Great Plague, 24
Greek Hermes, 17
Greenwich Mean Time, 27

H

Handshape, 162
Hangedman, the, 145, 176
Hare, the, 35
Headline, the, 165
Heartline, the, 164
Hearts, 185–6
Hermit, the, 144, 176
Hexagrams, 200–5
Hierophant, the, 175
High Priestess, the, 142, 174
Hindu Vedas, 18
Hitler, Adolf, 196
Horses, the, 35, 42
Hotels, 197
Houses, 28–29

I

I Ching, 199–205
Innin or Inanna, 14
    Lady of Heaven, 14
Iscariot, Judas , 1077
Ishtar, 14, 17
    Morning Star, 14
    Evening Star, 14

J

Judgement, 148
Jupiter, 14, 15, 30, 32, 53
    the Mount of, 167

Justice, 144, 176
Jyotisha Pandit, 18

K

Karma, 18

L

Lakes, 197
Last Supper, the, 177
Leo, 31, 50–2, 82–8, 83–5, 88
Libra, 31, 50, 96–102, 97–8,
    100, 102
Life line, the, 165
Lily, William, 24
Lincoln, Abraham, 196
Lithomancy, 9
Lovers, the, 143, 175
Luna, the Mount of, 167
Lychnomancy, 9

M

Magi, the, 19
Magician, the, 141, 174
Major Arcana, 139, 141,
    176–7
Marduk, 15
Mars, 14, 15, 30, 32, 53
    the Mount of, 167
Mayan manuscript, *15*
Mayas, 15
Meanings of numbers, 174–7
Melothesis, 19
Mercury, 14, 15, 30, 31, 32,
    52, 175
    the Mount of, 167
    the Line of, 169
Mesopotamia, 13, 14, 195
Mesopotamian astrology, 15
Minor Arcana, 139, 152
Minor Lines, the, 168–9

Mithraism, 19
Monkey, the, 35, 44
Moon, the, 21, 31, 52, 147,
    174–5
Moore, Francis, 24
Mounts, the, 166–7, *166*

N

Nabu, 17
Nakedness, 197
Name number, 172
Nastradamus, *6*
Necromancy, 157–9
Neptune, 30, 33, 53
Nergal, 15
NREM, 194
Numerology, 171–7

O

Odin, 10
Old Moore's Almanac, 24
Onychomancy *see* Finger
    nails
Ouija boards, 158–9, *159*
Ox, the, 35

P

Palm, the, 164
Palmistry, 161–9
Panchaga, 18
Paracelsus, 161
Pentacles, 155
Persian Gulf, 13
Phrenology, 207, 215, *215*
Pig, the, 35, 47
Pisces, 31, 50, 51, 53, 131–7,
    132–3, 135, 137
Planchettes, 158–9, *158–9*
Playing cards, *188*
Plotinus, 19

Pluto, 30, 33, 53
Ptolemy (Claudius
    Ptolemaeus), 16, *16*
Pyromancy, 207, 210

R
Rabbit, the, 35
Rat, the, 35, 36
REM, 194
Roman Mercury, 17
Rooster, the, 35, 45
Royal Spread, the, 149
Rubicon, 196
Rune
    positions, 10
    meanings, 10
Runes, 10

S
Saggittarius, 31, 50, 51, 53,
    110–16, *111–12, 114, 116*
Saturn, 14, 30, 32, 53, 176
    the Mount of, 167
Saturn Ninib, 15
Scorpio, 31, 50, 51, 53, 103–9,
    104–5, 107, 109, 114
Scribe Adda, *14*
Scrying, 179
Seven-Card Spread, 149
Shamash, 15
Sibley, Ebenezer, 24
Simple System, the, 189
Sin, the Moon God, 14
Snake, the, 35, 41
Sortilege, 212
Spades, 185, 187
Star, the, 147, 176
Stonehenge, 6
Strength, 144, 176
Sumer, 13, 15
Sumerians, 14

Sun, the, 20, 30, 52, 147, 174,
    176
Superstitions, 217–19
Swords, 154

T
Tarot, 138–148, *140*
    Tarot-reading techniques,
    149
    What the cards signify,
    150
    Reading interpreted, 151
Tasseomancy, 207, 208
Taurus, 22, 31, 50, 51, 61–7,
    62–3, 65, 67
Temperance, 146
Thehierophant (High Priest,
    143
Throwing dice, 212
Thumb, the, 164
Tibetan manuscript, 7
Tiger, the, 35, 38
Tower, the, 146
Trigrams, the, 200

U
Uranus, 30, 33, 53, 174
Ur of the Chaldees, 13
Using coffee grounds, 210
Using molten lead or wax,
    210
Using the circle, 213
Utu, 15

V
Venus, 14, 17, 30, 32, 52–3,
    175
    the Mount of, 167
Virgo, 31, 50–2, 89–95, *90–1,
    93, 95*
Vox Stellarum, 24

W
Wands, 152
Water signs, 50
Watt, James, 196
Weddings, 197
Western astrology, 21–33
Wheel of Fortune, the, 144,
    177
Whitman, Walt, 194
Woman with Child, The, 19
World, the, 148, 176

X
Astrology 6–7, *6–7*

Y
yin-yang, *17*, 200
    yang, 18
    yin, 18

Z
Zodiac, 21, 22, *23, 30*, 35, 49,
    50